W9-AJK-592

Living
the Lord's
Prayer

David Timms

Living the Lord's Prayer

David Timms

BETHANYHOUSE
MINNEAPOLIS, MINNESOTA

Published by Bethany House Publishers
11400 Hampshire Avenue South
Bloomington, Minnesota 55438

Bethany House Publishers is a
division of Baker Publishing Group, Grand Rapids, Michigan.

Printed in the United States of America

Library of Congress Cataloging-in-Publication Data

Timms, David.
    Living the Lord's prayer / David Timms.
        p.   cm.
    Summary: "Examines the Lord's Prayer as a simple but profound framework for the journey toward Christian maturity"—Provided by publisher.
    Includes bibliographical references.
    ISBN 978-0-7642-0506-4 (hardcover : alk. paper)   1. Lord's prayer—Criticism, interpretation, etc.   1. Title.

    BV230.T46   2008
    226.9'606—dc22

                                                                2008014106

To my parents, John and Pam Timms,
who have lived these words all of my life.

Our Father in the heavens,
hallowed be your name,
your kingdom come,
your will be done
on earth as it is in heaven.
Give us this day our daily bread.
Forgive us our debts,
as we also have forgiven our debtors.
And lead us not into testing,
but deliver us from the evil.
For yours is the kingdom,
the power, and the glory, forever. Amen.

(MATTHEW 6:9–13)

This is my own translation based on the Greek text.

Acknowledgments

It's misleading to place just one name on the cover of this book. A wonderful God-assembled community deserves recognition.

Tim Riter relentlessly pushed me to become a writer, and when this book took shape in my heart, he gave it a title. Kyle Duncan, Vice-President/Editorial at Bethany House, inspired me with his enthusiasm for the project. My LifeGroup (Kevin and Darcy, Keith and Tracy, Brent and Cynthia, Scott and Stephanie, Don and Sonia, Rob and Shannon, Gary and Carol) has listened to so many of these concepts and allowed me the space to air and explore them further. Gary and Carol also opened their mountain cabin as a writer's retreat for me. Scott and Stephanie devoted many hours to reading the manuscript and offering much needed guidance. The administration at Hope International University encouraged me to keep writing. Ellen Chalifoux, my editor at Bethany House, has critiqued and shaped the rough timbers into dressed ones. My sincerest and deepest thanks to each of you.

I also want to acknowledge my online community. Since January 2001, hundreds of folk—some of whom I know personally and most I do not—have graciously received my regular *In Hope* emails. That online community has allowed me to write often about the themes of this book and given feedback that has shaped it significantly.

A special thanks to my wife, Kim, who has always insisted that I have a writing voice and should use it. Her faith in Christ inspires me and her support of me to write on spiritual formation—when I have so far to grow in my own life— amazes me.

I did not assemble this community or the many other wonderful people in my life. All honor to the Father, the Son, and the Holy Spirit. "Yours is the kingdom, the power, and the glory, forever and ever."

Contents

Introduction

The Lord's Prayer and Spiritual Formation

In December 1911, Douglas Mawson, a twenty-nine-year-old Australian geologist and explorer, led a twenty-five-man scientific team to the frozen and forbidding tundra of eastern Antarctica. The team established a base at Commonwealth Bay and sent out small expeditionary parties. After a brutal winter at base camp, Mawson decided to explore the interior with two companions, a dog handler named Belgrave Ninnis and world ski champion Xavier Mertz.

The three men planned to travel twelve hundred miles across the largely uncharted territory, but the conditions proved far more arduous than expected. After six weeks, the men and their dogs had covered only three hundred miles. They decided to turn back, but that very day Ninnis, along with the six strongest dogs and the food sled, vanished into a crevasse. Mawson and Mertz had just a week's supply of food for themselves, no dog rations for their six remaining huskies, and a five-week journey ahead of them to return to Commonwealth Bay.

They set off, shooting the weakest dogs one by one for food as their hunger demanded. Mawson and Mertz noticed deep strips of their own skin peeling off, not realizing that the huskies' livers were poisoning them with toxic amounts of vitamin A. After three weeks—and still a long distance from the base camp—Mertz died.

Mawson pushed on. He made it to Aladdin's Cave, an outpost just five and a half miles from base camp, where fierce winds stranded him for a week. Finally the weather broke and Mawson made the steep hike down to camp. But he arrived too late. The ship sent to pick up his expedition had sailed away just six hours before. Remarkably, six men had waited in case Mawson returned, and they holed up in the camp with him until the ship came back for them—ten and a half months later.[1]

> *We want to know the deep interior things of God.*

We might marvel at such a story of courage, hunger, and survival. Yet those events a century ago reflect the spiritual journey for many of us. Just as Douglas Mawson could not be tied down to a mundane, ordinary life, many of us feel the same way about our spiritual lives. Surely God did not intend the abundant life to be drab, boring, empty, or tedious. We harbor deep suspicions that something deeper and vaster lies beyond our daily routines. We may not face howling winds and blistering cold or find ourselves stranded on the most desolate and isolated continent of the world, but many of us share the deep yearning to explore the spiritual realm more fully. We want to know the deep interior things of God. Along the way, we face a range of obstacles that stop some of us in our tracks. We find ourselves, at times, distracted—even poisoned—by things we thought were harmless. And then at the moment we feel like we've finally arrived home, we find that the ship has left with most of our friends.

The journey to know the heart of God can seem every bit as exhilarating and stretching as an Antarctic expedition. Thankfully, others have already explored and charted the territory. Christian men and women throughout the centuries have walked the Way ahead of us and left maps and markers, and Jesus has done it most clearly of all.

In the pages ahead, we'll examine some of their findings and discoveries. We'll walk behind them and explore places that perhaps we've not seen before. And we'll see how Jesus captures it all in the Lord's Prayer.

Not everyone wants to be an Antarctic explorer. It's easier and more comfortable to sit at home and let life pass by. Many of us prefer entertainment to exploration. But for those with a spirit of adventure and a hunger for the new, this book invites you to an old Journey. If you're willing to pack only the essentials and pursue the wonderful interior places of faith, we'll get underway.

A Shared Hunger

Our quest has a long history. For centuries Christian men and women have desired a deeper walk with God. The desert hermits of Egypt in the second and third centuries went to extreme measures in their pursuit of God. Some secluded themselves for years in caves. Others, known as stylites, lived long periods perched on tall poles. Can you imagine? Have you met any pole-sitters recently? They believed that withdrawal from a decadent society could propel them into divine intimacy. They too wanted to know God and change their world. But the hot deserts, lonely caves, and strange locations generally failed to yield the secrets of the deeper Christian life. The harsh environment by itself could not deepen the heart of a person.

For two thousand years various Christian mystics and devout believers have advocated a range of pathways to a deeper relationship with God. They shared our hunger for the holy.

> *The spiritual life should not be treated lightly.*

Benedict of Nursia,[2] one of the early spiritual pioneers, established a monastery and wrote his *Rule* to guide fellow monks to the heart of God. He insisted on seriousness, obedience, and humility as the three pillars for intimacy with the Lord. The spiritual life should not be treated lightly. Centuries later Bernard of Clairvaux[3] found himself transfixed and transformed by the love of Christ. He preferred passion instead of rigid discipline and taught that Christian maturity emerges from an encounter with divine love. What contrasting pathways.

Julian of Norwich[4] wrote of her deepest yearning, to share the afflictions of Christ. She believed the *via dolorosa* ("the way of suffering") would usher in mystical union. At about the same time, Catherine of Sienna[5] used the metaphor of a bridge to describe the Christian journey. These women shared the same heart but very different approaches.

St. John of the Cross[6] struggled to reconcile God's nearness with his own feelings of spiritual dryness. His *Dark Night of the Soul* explored the purging work of God in our lives. Simultaneously, Teresa of Avila[7] addressed the deeper Christian life through her book *The Interior Castle,* in which she compared the journey of faith with entering more and more privileged courts within a castle. St. John explained spiritual formation in terms of testing, while Teresa described it in terms of privilege.

Shortly thereafter, the Catholic Church confiscated and burned the writings of Madam Guyon[8] because she proposed "praying the Scriptures" and encouraged the common people to listen to the Lord. Her suggestion could have put the clergy out of business! A century later, and across the English Channel, John Wesley[9] believed spiritual awakening sprung from Bible study, and he strongly urged folk to immerse themselves in the Word.

At the turn of the twentieth century (1906), Pentecostalism erupted from Azusa Street in Los Angeles. This movement framed the deeper Christian life in terms of ecstatic experience and sensitivity to the Spirit of God.

Dietrich Bonhoeffer,[10] martyred at Flossenburg Concentration Camp at the end of World War II, decried cheap grace and urged his readers to a radical commitment to Christ and the Christian community. We cannot be one with God and only half-hearted about Christ or the body of Christ.

Twenty years later Thomas Merton,[11] a Trappist monk, wrote prolifically, calling Christians to contemplative prayer and social engagement. And Henri Nouwen,[12] who died in 1996, became a surrogate spiritual director for countless thousands of believers through his writings. In them, he insisted that intimacy with God emerges from belovedness and brokenness.

If we summarize these saints of the past, we develop quite a catalog of possible pathways. We draw nearer to God through:

- Seriousness, obedience, and humility

- Spiritual disciplines of silence, solitude, fasting, study, and more

- Encountering the love of God

- Sharing the sufferings of Christ

- Crossing metaphorical bridges and entering metaphorical castles

- Enduring the purging work of God in our lives

- Praying the Scriptures

- Studying the Scriptures

- Spiritual gifts and revivalism

- Devotion to the body of Christ

- Meditative prayer and social engagement

- Belovedness and brokenness

Assessing the Options

This brief scan of history neglects a host of other great and influential thinkers like St. Augustine, Brother Lawrence, SørenKierkegaard, Frank Laubach, Martin Luther, Thomas à Kempis, Francis of Assisi, John Chrysostom, and George Fox. But our brief survey shows that sincere believers have ventured down considerably different paths in pursuit of the same goal: closeness to the Father. Their suggestions and experiences range from spiritual disciplines to spiritual encounters. Each one offers earnest, sincere, and authentic insights, and while their reflections merit our prayerful attention, they raise several questions.

First, does their diversity have a common denominator? Second, are these suggestions explicitly *Christian*? Third, can we collate the tremendous insights of the ages in one place?

The vast array of insights inspire, but also confuse us. Every tidbit of wisdom sounds good and right, but without a fixed point of reference we become rudderless in a sea of generic spirituality. Our hearts resonate with those who have walked close to God, but we lack the experience or wisdom to accurately assess their advice.

A fixed reference point does exist— in Scripture.

Nevertheless, a fixed reference point does exist—in Scripture. We find a ready-made summary not in the saints or scholars of the past, but in Christ himself.

The Lord's Prayer

Jesus lays out what we commonly call the Lord's Prayer, and in it He provides the greatest Christian teaching of the centuries on spiritual formation. The Prayer exceeds simple passion or fancy rhetoric. It incorporates and reveals some of the most profound spiritual truths of the kingdom of God. Jesus does not borrow His words from any cultural clichés of the first century. His phrases transcend the ordinary fare heard in synagogues of that day.

More than a prayer, the Lord's Prayer outlines the most fundamental features of the deeper Christian life. Long before the desert hermits and the medieval mystics, Christ himself laid out the pathway to spiritual fulfillment. He did so with a startling economy of words, but with clarity that still speaks to those of us weary of the cheap wisdom of our day and desiring genuine intimacy with God.

Just when we might expect lengthy explanations of the mysterious, Jesus uses just seventy-two words,[13] and in those few words He outlines life-giving attitudes and paradigms. We also encounter a prayer that does not seek to get God's attention but to give our attention to Him. Barbara Brown Taylor notes:

> Our corporate prayers are punctuated with phrases such as "Hear us, Lord" or "Lord, hear our prayer," as if the burden to listen were on God and not us. We name our concerns, giving God suggestions on what to do about them. What reversal of power might occur if we turned

the process around, naming our concerns and asking God to tell us what to do about them? "Speak, Lord, for your servants are listening."[14]

The Lord's Prayer definitely guides us into a "reversal of power" and turns around the process of both our prayers and our lives.

Luke recalls the Lord's Prayer in its shortened form. Matthew records the longer version. In Matthew 6:9–13, the Prayer appears as a centerpiece to the majestic Sermon on the Mount.

The Prayer functions less as a chant and more as a challenge. The words seem deceptively simple. Memorizing ten short lines poses little difficulty for most of us. But the concepts and insights

> *The Prayer has the capacity to remold our lives entirely.*

have the capacity to remold our lives entirely. Overstatement? Exaggeration? Not at all. Indeed, as we'll see, this prayer offers a simple framework that steers us through all the suggestions of the ages and into the very intimacy with Christ that our hearts desire. It reveals the building blocks for authentic spiritual formation.

Spiritual Formation

We frequently hear the phrase *spiritual formation* in Western Christian culture, but its meaning generally remains obscure. What does spiritual formation really involve? What does the final product really look like? Some believers use the term *Christlikeness* and suggest that if we show greater compassion today than yesterday, we're on the right track. In other words, formation has to do with character. Others reserve the phrase *spiritual formation* to describe the process of becoming otherworldly or learning to speak in a spiritual jargon.

Wil Hernandez provides a helpful definition. He describes spiritual formation as "the process of being with Christ in order to become like Christ and consequently live for Christ."[15] His succinct definition captures three vital elements. Did you notice them?

- Being with Christ

- Becoming like Christ

- Living for Christ

Spiritual formation is not *one* or even *two* of these three elements. True formation, as modeled by Jesus and reflected in the Prayer, incorporates some measure of all three parts of the definition. Spiritual formation remains incomplete when it becomes fixated on meditation ("being with"). But it also fails when it focuses entirely on character adjustment or behavior modification ("becoming like"). Similarly, the process falters if it simply means busyness in the kingdom ("living for").

Imagine for a moment someone who prays earnestly, faithfully, and constantly but who continues to cheat those around them. It would rightly arouse our suspicions. Something is deeply wrong. Similarly, consider the person who undergoes an anger management course and learns new life skills through counseling. They seem happier and more willing to volunteer for service in the church. However, if they know nothing about the abiding presence of Christ, and neither speak of Him nor read His Word, we might praise them for the turnaround in their life, but few of us will label them a "spiritual example." We intuitively know that authentic spiritual formation must percolate through every aspect of our lives. It flows from a three-part foundation: being with Christ, becoming like Christ, and living for Christ.

The teaching contained in the Lord's Prayer catapults us toward complete transformation. While we soak up the wisdom of godly men and women throughout Christian history, they would certainly defer to the wisdom of Christ expressed in the Prayer.

Thus throughout the next eleven chapters, we'll explore the basic elements of the Lord's Prayer. And as we revisit the Prayer, reading it closely and contemplatively, we'll unwrap principles that nourish the deeper Christian life and point the way to the deepest walk with God.

Ultimately, the Lord's Prayer reveals more about how to live than how to pray.

CHAPTER 1

$=====$ Our $=====$

Committing to Community

In *A Painted House,* John Grisham captures our curiosity with his opening line: "The hill people and the Mexicans arrived on the same day. It was a Wednesday, early in 1952."[1] Immediately the imagery and details transport us to another time and place and introduce people who intrigue us. It compels us to read on.

Similarly, Charles Dickens began his famous 1859 historical novel *A Tale of Two Cities* with tantalizing words:

It was the best of times, it was the worst of times, it was the age of wisdom, it was the age of foolishness, it was the epoch of belief, it was the epoch of incredulity, it was the season of Light, it was the season of Darkness, it was the spring of hope, it was the winter of despair, we had everything before us, we had nothing before us, we were all going direct to heaven, we were all going direct the other way.[2]

The contrasts demand our immediate engagement. We don't drift into the story. We're driven into it.

In much the same way, the opening words of the Lord's Prayer have special force. Jesus begins with two words—just nine letters in Greek or English—that send shudders through any of us who value individualism and independence; two small words that challenge our common experience.

Our Father becomes not just an introductory formula, as though we need to start somewhere. It does not serve the same function as *Dear God*. Rather, this short phrase launches us into new territory.

At first it doesn't seem so. Some of us have uttered those words so frequently and so casually over a lifetime that we fail to recognize the power they contain. Rote repetition dulls us to their life-shaping potential. But if we'll pause, we'll discover that *Our Father* calls and invites us to new places—the ground zero of spiritual formation.

In this chapter, let's consider the significance of the short pronoun *our*.

Society and Community

A *Washington Post* article, in June 2006, reported:

Americans are far more socially isolated today than they were two decades ago, and a sharply growing number of

people say they have no one in whom they can confide. . . .
A quarter of Americans say they have no one with whom
they can discuss personal troubles, more than double the
number who were similarly isolated in 1985.[3]

Lynn Smith-Lovin, a Duke University sociologist who
helped conduct the study, noted that people may have six hundred friends on Facebook and email twenty-five people a day,
but rarely discuss matters of personal importance.

Western culture is adrift. At some point in the past, we left
the moorings of community and settled for society. The shift
has had profound implications. *Society* speaks to our ability to
organize ourselves as a group of people. *Community* speaks to
our connectedness to one another. *Society* refers to structures
and systems. *Community* refers to relationships. The two terms
share common ground—people—but their commonality stops
there. A stronger society does not necessarily produce a stronger
community. For example, a well-oiled Little League Baseball club
(a sporting *society*), with weekly email contact and automated
phone reminders of upcoming events, carefully planned game
schedules, and smooth administration does not automatically
produce camaraderie among parents and goodwill among play-
ers. As a group of people with a mutual interest in baseball they
may have a strong *society* but relatively weak *community*. Many
people within that society get a service they want, but may barely
know each other. The club (society) has rules that tell people
how to report misbehavior, fulfill team responsibilities, collect
sponsorship, and treat umpires. But a *community* requires more

than policies and procedures. Indeed, community cannot be legislated with bylaws or constructed with a constitution.

In short, we have generally failed to build community and, instead, settled for society. The upshot of this failure is social isolation. We function satisfactorily with many people but have virtually no meaningful connection with any of them.

We need not dwell on the multiple and complex factors that produce this social isolation. Suffice to note that most of us have grown up in it and have grown accustomed to it. Indeed, one evidence of our inclination to prefer society over community is that we've learned to resort more to *systems* rather than rely on *people.* If someone injures us, we immediately consider lawsuit options through the courts. We use judicial, political, educational, medical, and financial *systems* to our advantage if at all possible. We no longer negotiate firsthand with people but thirdhand (I will speak to my lawyer who will speak to your lawyer who will speak to you), and we insist that the various systems protect our personal rights. All of this breeds a culture absorbed by personal rights rather than collective good, something that reflects a strong society and a weak community.

In the midst of such relational ineptitude—true in the days of Jesus and true in our own day—the opening word of the Prayer has explosive force.

You, Me, and Us

Our. This tiny word forms an immediate bridge between *you* and *me.* It speaks of a shared experience and a shared ownership. It speaks of community. *Me* and *mine* produces isolation and aloneness. So does *you* and *your*. But the unifying *our* produces an entirely different dynamic. The Prayer starts strategically.

> Our. *This tiny word forms an immediate bridge between* you *and* me.

Our. Is any word more profoundly needed today, or more commonly absent? The possessiveness of the two-year-old tugging mightily on his toy while his friend holds on with equal determination becomes a lifelong characteristic for too many of us. Perhaps herein lies the wisdom of Christ.

Spiritual writers throughout the ages have noted that the journey to a deeper walk with God can only be fully lived in the company of God's people. Dietrich Bonhoeffer wrote:

> Let him who cannot be alone beware of community. He will only do harm to himself and to the community. . . . But the reverse is also true: Let him who is not in community beware of being alone. . . . Each by itself has profound pitfalls and perils. One who wants fellowship without solitude plunges into the void of words and feelings, and the one who seeks solitude without fellowship perishes in the abyss of vanity, self-infatuation, and despair.[4]

Early believers could not conceive of "personal Christian faith." The only way to think of oneself was in the context of others. The corporate model prevailed. Indeed, the apostle Paul generally used the plural form of *you* in his epistles, not as a means to address many separate individuals, but as a device to emphasize the unity of the body—the togetherness and inclusiveness of everyone in this new kingdom context. Any effort to isolate ourselves from each other violates the integrity of the body. Of course, the temptation to withdraw and form our own spirituality is strong, especially when relationships present so much potential for conflict and hurt. Would it not be easier to have the character of Christ if we could form it apart from the irritations of others?

But spirituality formed in a relational vacuum turns out to be hollow. It may have all the appearance of something large and colorful but it contains little substance. God does not dwell beyond life, but in the midst of it. We may find His presence equally on the mountaintop and in the management meeting. Real formation may happen in the middle of the night with a crying child as much as on a solitary retreat to a stained-glass chapel. Here's why *our* becomes such a crucial starting point. Whenever we abandon the body, we undermine ourselves.

Community and Stability

St. Benedict, sometimes described as the father of Western monasticism, knew this. He lived early in the sixth century, when monks complained about each other and grew restless within their communities. The brothers found themselves in conflict and frequently traveled in search of new monasteries more conducive to their spiritual formation. In such an environment, Benedict added a new element to the traditional vows of poverty, chastity, and obedience. He insisted that those who wanted to grow deeply in Christ should also take a vow of stability.[5]

With this vow of stability, Benedict attempted to reestablish the priority of *us* over *me* in spiritual formation. He knew very well that grace could only flourish when it encountered offense; forgiveness requires conflict; healing emerges from hurt; and strength arises from struggle. Thus, the pathway to true spiritual formation demands long-term engagement with others in community. When times get tough, we don't run. Neither do we simply battle it out. Rather, we learn to resolve and reconcile.

Benedict's ancient call for people to put down roots and learn the give-and-take of community has never been more relevant. The nomadic lifestyles of various cultural groups throughout history have reached unprecedented levels in Western culture today. In 2005–2006, about 14 percent of all U.S. residents moved— nearly 40 million people.[6] Consider how many different homes you have lived in, different jobs you have held, different churches you have attended, and different groups you have served.

In my own story, by my mid-forties I had lived in eleven different homes, held at least nine different jobs (with different businesses, churches, or institutions), attended nine different schools, and participated short-term in countless clubs and organizations. Most people throughout human history could not fathom such a résumé, yet I suspect that my experience looks stable compared to many of my peers.

No wonder then that *our* becomes a difficult concept to genuinely embrace. The only stable part of my life experience is *my*, which I take with me everywhere. When the *us* keeps changing, it's natural to nurture a personal and private spirituality for the only constant—*me.* This makes Benedict's ancient caution resoundingly relevant. We cannot grow in grace by withdrawing from others.

Beyond Personality

We must also understand that personality does not determine our community involvement. Before we sigh and hand off spiritual formation to the extroverts around us—those who get their energy from other people and naturally gravitate to an *our* kind of lifestyle—let's clearly understand that *our* denotes an inclusive mentality and a commitment to engagement. Any commitment we make to community does not require that we become bubbly, effervescent, and always-on-call. Nor does it mean that we must always agree to every request or plan. We need boundaries that create space for building special friendships, experiencing personal rejuvenation, and nurturing our own walk with Christ. However, this first word of the Prayer—*our*—reinforces the fundamental communal aspect of the kingdom.

While some of us may prefer a more private existence, perhaps even praying, "My Father," the Prayer calls us to a corporate life, a life shared with others, a life in which God works through each of us to bless each of us.

Wendy found it difficult to work with others. Her intense task-orientation meant that she found little joy in the idle chatter that others seemed to love. Furthermore, they worked slowly and sloppily by her perfectionist standards. Ever since junior high she had hated group projects and felt the same way in her adulthood. Yes, she performed at remarkably high levels. The quality and quantity of her work impressed everyone. But at a cost. And that cost had both relational and spiritual elements. Her high demands and expectations isolated her from people. Team environments frustrated her and project partners found her quietly intolerant and critical. With time this pattern became a performance-based lifestyle that also hindered a grace-based walk with the Father.

Wendy came to place higher value on productivity than relationships. This made her a valued member of society but fairly indifferent to community, as we've already defined those terms. But this independence and perfectionism contained a more sinister element. When productivity becomes the driving force of our own lives, we begin to view and evaluate other people in terms of their productivity. Without even realizing it, we value people not as human beings but as workers or performers. We grow blind to their humanity and see them, basically, as machinery.

Human Machinery

We pierce our souls—turning life into mere existence—when we view people primarily as commodities. The culture around us constantly diminishes humanity, and we see indications of this change even in the language of the marketplace.

In the business world we no longer have "personnel" but "human resources." We reduce living and loving beings to the status of breathing machines. In our present culture all of us find that we are studied, named, and treated as functions and things.

We *network* with each other. Isn't that a computer term for how machines hook together to function more efficiently? Everyone is a potential buyer for what we sell, student for what we teach, member for the church, recruit for the ministry, or resource for a task that needs to be done.

The faddish emphasis on spiritual gifts in our day—as never before in human history—emerges from our contemporary infatuation with usefulness and functionality. We measure a person's value by their capacity to perform. People exist, it seems, to fulfill a higher purpose—usually numerical (how many?), architectural (how big?), or monetary (how much?) in nature. And in such a utilitarian environment, we feel pressured to make a spiritual contribution. We fit in,

> *We measure a person's value by their capacity to perform.*

we're told, because of a role we play or a ministry we do. The gurus of spiritual gifts then administer surveys and instruments to help us identify our role or function in the body, and we expect to find fulfillment and satisfaction with such a discovery. Could anything be more counter-gospel?

Future historians will undoubtedly earmark our age for its glaring depersonalization. We fragment the family unit in order to improve our productivity. Consequently, children are left to baby-sitters, preschool care, and after-school care so that both parents might pursue productive careers. We consign our parents to aged-care facilities because we have neither the time nor the confidence to *do life* with them in their declining years. Because we struggle with meaningful relationships, we gravitate to manageable and seemingly safe tasks (careers), and in the process we treat each other more as commodities than companions.

Consider also the pride we take in terms like *driven* and *task-oriented*. These words have become complimentary. They make us feel good about ourselves. They make us feel important and needed. As a culture, we also attach inordinate honor to the word *achiever*—so much so that *achiever* has preferred status over *lover* or *friend*.

When we view people from this mechanistic mindset, we drain away the essence of life itself. When production, doing, achieving, and organizing is the *essence* of our lives, then love becomes either an inconvenience or a plain nuisance—in marriage, family, church, or workplace.

As long as results trump relationships, we embrace the cultural shift from human beings to human machinery. And in the process, we deny the most fundamental reality of our humanity; that we are made in the image of God—the Lover, the Friend, the Relational One.

Jesus rarely seemed hurried or harried. He stopped counting at twelve, and never called the disciples His team members. He called them friends, and lived like it. For Him, *our* had an intensely personal ring to it.

The Pain and Pleasure of *Our*

We should not speak too cavalierly about the word *our*, as though it is an innocuous concept that we have simply overlooked or outgrown. Quite the contrary. *Our* has fallen from the cultural vocabulary not because of its insipidity but because it's like a beaker of nitroglycerin in the hands of a child.

We live in a period in history when *our* has become both tantalizing and tormenting. We desperately want connection with each other but also deeply fear it. The proliferation of pain from broken homes, failed marriages, abusive experiences, and profound loneliness creates both desire for and deep anxiety about intimacy.

On the one hand, we long for strong connection with each other. I attended a wedding ceremony in a building with seats arranged in rows. Each row had five separate padded seats pushed together. I watched with amusement as a group of junior-highers squeezed eight bodies on a single row, with empty seats a row in front and a row behind. Togetherness

> *Togetherness forms part of our God-designed emotional DNA.*

matters a lot to us, and while we may conceal our needs as we grow older, we cannot deny them. It forms part of our God-designed emotional DNA.

As a youngster, I enjoyed playing cricket and rugby—not because I stood out as a great athlete but because I loved the team camaraderie. In the sporting context, *our* can produce enormous satisfaction; shared goals, dreams, and efforts. We live and relive great moments of connectedness with others.

On the other hand, our inexperience or failure at intimacy—something that seems so painless on TV—intimidates us and keeps us from pursuing it further. None of us enjoys rejection. Consequently, we may find ourselves withdrawing into a voluntary seclusion to avoid the pain of being let down (again) by someone.

When we get hurt, *our* feels dangerous. Divorce can make us wary of intimacy. Abuse can make us fearful of togetherness. And fear of God's punishment can make us nervous about pursuing Him. Yet as David Benner writes, "In spite of the messages of Western culture, personal fulfillment lies in connection, not autonomy. Spirituality is the discovery of the fundamental connection that exists between us and God."[7]

The language of *our*, then, becomes both inviting and threatening. It invites us to fulfillment and threatens us with failure. In the midst of these mixed emotions, we may tentatively join with other believers, but we generally prefer to do so without making any binding commitments.

Virtual Community

Shane Hipps discusses the rise and apparent popularity of virtual community through the electronic media today. He writes:

In virtual community, our contacts involve very little real risk and demand even less of us personally. In this sense we experience the paradox of *intimate anonymity.* [This virtual community] functions a bit like cotton candy: it goes down easy and satiates our immediate hunger, but it doesn't provide much in the way of sustainable nutrition. It spoils our appetite for the kind of authentic community to which Scripture calls us. . . . If virtual community functions like cotton candy, then authentic community is more like broccoli. It may not always taste good but it provides crucial nourishment for the formation of our identity. Authentic community will undoubtedly be marked by conflict, risk, and rejection. At the same time it offers the deepest levels of acceptance, intimacy, and support.[8]

Virtual community declares *mine* and *yours* and *his* and *hers* as though everyone lives independent lives linked only by a thread or two. But genuine community demands an authentic, collective, inclusive *our*—multiple lives woven strongly together, not simply hanging by threads.

Prayer itself becomes a corporate act—no longer *me and God* but *us and God.* And more than that, each of us with one another *and* with God. It affirms our commitment to be attentive to both the horizontal and vertical lines of relationship, to both the external and the internal forces of our lives. It dismisses any personal agenda and draws us into a gathering of speakers and listeners and saints, past and present, who collectively belong to each other and to God.

We dare go no further in spiritual formation until we decide, once and for all, firmly and unreservedly, that we cannot love God if we do not love our brother (1 John 4:20); that we cannot be one with Him if we disregard the unity of His body (Ephesians 4:3–6); that we cannot know the fellowship of the Trinity except that we enter fully into the Christian community (Philippians 2:1–2).

The illusion of the virtual community will reap the wind in generations to come because it presumes that intimacy is compatible with anonymity. The two terms, however, remain mutually exclusive. While email enables us to control the conversation—answering only what we want to answer when we want to answer it and with as much or little detail as we like—we evade real encounters that incorporate loads of nonverbal language and wrest control from us. Authentic relationships cannot be formed in a virtual environment. At some point, we must lower all masks and surrender all controls whereby we may truly know and be known. Such is the power of *our* as it escapes our lips at the start of the Prayer.

A Mantra

What greater way could Christ have started the Prayer?[9] In a single word He calls us together. Many Christians and many congregations would benefit from making this solitary word their mantra and mission. A mantra is simply a commonly repeated word or phrase that drives home a message or helps keep us focused on a certain truth.[10]

It would surely help defuse division if we recited endlessly that single affirmation: *Our*. When a friend fails us, the word *our* reminds us of our desire and commitment to live in grace and forgiveness. When a neighbor wounds or irritates us, *our* beckons us to remain neighborly. When we gather for worship, *our* helps us focus on the collective experience, not just my personal preference. When the first-grade boys get rambunctious during Sunday school, *our* reinforces the high importance of their being there. When our spouse hurts us, *our* revives the vows we took on our wedding day. When a fellow believer lies dying of cancer, *our* produces empathy as we see his struggle as part of our own mortality.

> *Each time we use the word* our, *we assert our commitment to remain together.*

Each time we use the word *our,* we assert our commitment to remain together, we recognize the importance of community, and we affirm a spiritual formation opportunity.

The Christian community provides not only the place for our spiritual growth but also the impetus for it.

When I was a young man, I enjoyed hiking and camping. Nothing compared with making damper—an Australian bread—on the last night of a trip. We'd mix the flour, water, and other ingredients and let the dough sit on a rock near the fire so it could rise a little. Meanwhile, we pulled aside a number of coals to let them cool. After perhaps thirty minutes for the dough to rise, we'd dig open the fire and make a hole in the center of it right down to the ground. Into that hole we plopped the dough. We'd place the cooled coals directly on the bread, and then cover everything with the hottest coals that were left. The bread would stay in that little "oven" for an hour or so, before we rolled it out with a stick, scraped off the embedded coals and ash, broke it open, and feasted on it. A hiker's delight! But to get a good damper, we had to keep the coals together. One coal could not cook the damper, no matter how hot that coal was. In isolation the coals lost their heat and effectiveness. But together, and with fire from above, they produced a delectable result.

Our binds us together. It becomes the glue between all believers. It jolts us to recall that we stand together before God with all His children—equally, interdependently, without favoritism or exception. *Our* levels the playing field. It erases distinctions, labels, and status issues. It renders us the same. *My* excludes others. *Our* is the language of inclusion.

> Our *is the language of inclusion.*

Parker Palmer noted:

> If we are to grow as persons . . . we must consciously participate in the emerging community of our lives, in the claims made upon us by others as well as our claims upon them. Only in community does the person appear in the first place, and only in community can the person continue to become.[11]

The End of Status

If Jesus pounded away on any kingdom principle, He pounded on equality. The kingdom of God has no room for status-hunting.

> Within minutes [Jesus' disciples] were bickering over who of them would end up the greatest. But Jesus intervened: "Kings like to throw their weight around and people in authority like to give themselves fancy titles. It's not going to be that way with you. Let the senior among you become like the junior; let the leader act the part of the servant."
>
> Luke 22:24 THE MESSAGE

The *our* of the Prayer does not distinguish between classes or categories. Jesus does not say, "Our—that is, those of us who are strong, competent, reliable, achievers. . . ." Nor does He imply that *our* relates to the clergy or the educated. The *our* includes everyone and implicitly acknowledges the level playing field among us. The apostle Paul would later be quite explicit in his interpretation of Jesus' teaching. He wrote unequivocally, "There is neither Jew nor Greek, slave nor free, male nor female, for you are all one in Christ Jesus" (Galatians 3:28).

The little prayer-word *our* calls us back to others. It forces *me* to consider *us*. *Me and God* creates a cocoon that isolates me from others and, ironically, from Him. *Us and the Father* reinforces the indispensability of the community.

CHAPTER 2

Father

Experiencing Love and Security

The statistics for homelessness in the United States continue to grow at an alarming rate. The United States Department of Health and Human Services estimates that "over a five-year period, about 2–3 percent of the U.S. population (5–8 million people) will experience at least one night of homelessness."[1] Imagine the entire populations of Atlanta, Chicago, Baltimore, Denver, Dallas, and one or two other cities—homeless.[2] Futhermore, the average age of a homeless person is nine, and families account for nearly 40 percent of the homeless numbers.[3]

However, if homelessness presents a challenge, the problem of lovelessness poses an even greater threat to society. We see symptoms of lovelessness, for example, in the rate of reported domestic violence, which has escalated dramatically in recent decades. In the United States, 5.3 million women are abused each year,[4] and nearly one in three American women reports being physically or sexually abused by a husband or boyfriend at some point in her life.[5]

Everywhere we look we see displaced and neglected people. Then, beyond the millions of discarded and abandoned souls, we encounter millions of others who live their lives in terrible isolation and loneliness.

Harvard professor Robert Putnam's ground-breaking book *Bowling Alone* stirred the conscience of America in 2001, when he showed that we sign fewer petitions, belong to fewer organizations that meet, know our neighbors less, socialize with friends less frequently, and even get together with our families less often.[6] Latchkey kids return to empty homes each day from school, and our electronic culture entertains us without meaningful social interaction. These experiences, among others, contribute to the growing alienation that we sense.

Abba, Father, and Israel

In this context, the second word of the Prayer provides a stark contrast to our common experience. *Father.* In Aramaic the term is *Abba*, a term of intimacy and respectful familiarity, a word of belonging and connection, of family and protection, and of love.

Unlike the familiar prayers of our day that often begin with the generic and impersonal words "Dear God," Jesus immediately challenges the preconceptions of His first hearers by teaching them to pray, "Our *Father.*" There's nothing generic or impersonal about this invocation, though our own familiarity with the Prayer may dull our sensitivity to its scandal.

In ancient Israel, Yahweh (God) remained unapproachable. No one dared utter His personal name. Indeed, when reading Scripture aloud, the Israelites preferred—and still do—to substitute various alternatives rather than possibly offend Him with mispronunciation. After all, to take His name in vain would violate the third commandment, and who's to know if that might include offending God by uttering His name with an incorrect inflection. The God of Israel, the Lord, the Holy One, remained transcendent. Only those He invited closer could draw near to Him. For example, the Lord called Moses to the top of Mount Sinai so He could speak to him (Exodus 19:20), and the High Priest was permitted to enter the Holy of Holies on the Day of Atonement (Leviticus 16). But no one in Israel would have expected or dared speak of a "personal relationship with God." Such familiarity was unimaginable.

Thus, when Jesus opened the Prayer with the intimate greeting *Father,* it must have startled His hearers. Although the Old Testament includes references to the fatherhood of God over both Israel and the King (for example, Exodus 4:22–23; Psalm 89:26), the references remain few and far between.

N. T. Wright observes:

> The first occurrence in the Hebrew Bible of the idea of God as the Father comes when Moses marches in boldly to stand before Pharoah, and says: Thus says YHWH: Israel is my son, my firstborn; let my people go, that they may serve me (Exodus 4:22–23). For Israel to call God

"Father," then, was to hold on to the hope of liberty. The slaves were called to be sons.[7]

We might easily hear strong undertones of deliverance in the Prayer that Jesus taught. The oppressed Jews of Jesus' first-century audience very possibly would have heard *Father* in terms of liberation and freedom from oppression as they recalled the Moses story. Just as God had delivered ancient Israel from Egypt, so Jesus may have implied in the Prayer that God would also deliver the Jews of His day from the oppressive Romans.

Wright's connection between father and freedom rings true. However, it does not negate the tone of intimacy inherent in the title. This opening greeting suggested a resoundingly new and fairly shocking level of intimacy.

Father—The Invitation to Love

Father denotes intimacy. In a healthy family environment—even in ancient Israel—a father's love formed the center of the household. Good fathers provided security not only in terms of physical safety but also emotional health.

> Father *denotes intimacy.*

The Old Testament has no Hebrew word that corresponds precisely to our English word *family.* Perhaps the closest equivalent is the phrase *bet ab,* which means "father's house," or the term *bayit* ("household"), which usually had a father's name associated with it (see Joshua 7:18). In the patriarchal society, the father dominated the family structure not only in power but also in responsibility. The father would be responsible to train his sons as they matured (Deuteronomy 4:9), decide inheritance (Genesis 27:1-4), and pronounce blessings (Genesis 49).

Jesus saw that the father's love sets the tempo for family relationships. He observed:

> Which of you fathers, if your son asks for a fish, will give him a snake instead? Or if he asks for an egg, will give him a scorpion? If you then, though you are evil, know how to give good gifts to your children, how much more will your Father in heaven give the Holy Spirit to those who ask him!
>
> Luke 11:11–13

When we call God *Father,* we affirm something very foundational about Him and about us. He protects and nurtures us as His beloved children. His Fatherhood and our childhood are opposite sides of the same coin.

Joel, my youngest son, came to me as a young child. He had a twinkle in his eye and the hint of a smile. "David, can I ask you something?" he said. It's a little disorienting to hear a six-year-old use your given name. Whoa! I stopped him in his tracks. He did not intend to insult or dishonor me. Joel's use of my given name had no disrespect in it, nor did it offend me. But there's a good reason for him not to use my first name. He has access to a name for me that only two other people in the world (his two brothers) can use: *Dad.* Why would he opt for a generic name, when he could use a special name that only a beloved child could use?

Similarly, when we refer to God as *Father* we express an implicit truth: He loves us dearly. Our own spiritual formation and growth always begins with God's unquenchable love for us.

The apostle John put it this way, "This is love: not that we loved God, but that he loved us and sent his Son as an atoning sacrifice for our sins" (1 John 4:10). Then, lest we miss the point, John reiterates it just nine verses later: "We love because he first loved us."

Jesus himself taught that the Father's love forms the central tenet of the kingdom. The renowned story of the prodigal ("extravagantly wasteful") son in Luke 15 could easily be re-titled the story of the prodigal father.

The son, who earlier demanded his share of the family inheritance, squanders everything and finds himself in the most desperate state imaginable for a Jew—eating pigs' food with the pigs. He plans to return to his father's home as a servant, clearly unworthy to be a son but desperate to live. And on the way home, he rehearses his speech. He imagines that he'll need to demonstrate his abject humility, apologize profusely, and beg for a place among the servants. After frittering away half the family estate, what else could he expect? Yet as Jesus tells the story, when the boy approaches the depleted homestead, his father sees him from a distance and rushes to greet him. He falls head over heels at the sight of his son.

The son begins his speech of contrition and repentance, but the father wants none of it. He seems deaf to the son's rehearsed lines. Instead, he gives hasty instructions to the servants to go and get the best robe they can find, and a ring, and some sandals. The father wants to lavish his love on the son *before the son even has a chance to explain himself.*

Jesus' use of the father figure in this story is not to highlight power, authority, or deliverance, but love. The father seems extravagantly wasteful with his love. And those who really hear the story have no doubt that the father's love forms the centerpiece of the narrative.

> *The temptation for many of us is to misjudge the Father's love.*

The temptation for many of us is to duplicate the mistake of the young son and misjudge the Father's love.

Father or Judge

The image of God as Father seems natural to many of us. However, we often fail to integrate our orthodoxy ("right opinions") with orthopraxy ("right actions"). We believe that He is a loving Father, but act as though He's a calculating judge. The weight we assign to these two different images will often determine whether or not we live under law or grace.

We constantly live under the burden of rules and regulations, always telling ourselves what we must, should, need to, have to, and ought to do. The demands are relentless. We should be better parents, ought to give more time to our neighbors, need to serve more in the church, have to restart our quiet time, and must be more compassionate. The list of demands stretches out endlessly.

We know that one day we shall stand before God and give an account for every word and deed in our lives. We desperately want to hear those reassuring words, "Well done, good and faithful servant! You have been faithful with a few things; I will put you in charge of many things. Come and share your master's happiness!" (Matthew 25:23). In other words, we accept our adoption into the family of God but see ourselves more as servants than family members.

When we became Christians, we responded to the gospel promise of freedom. But many of us then slipped into a church culture of duties and obligations. We celebrate the new covenant, and rejoice that salvation does not depend on our keeping the 613 commandments found throughout the Old Testament. But the further we journey in faith, the more we realize that perhaps we subtly replaced the old commandments with a raft of new ones: "Thou shalt tithe, be punctual, attend every service, be a part of a small group, be devoted to the corporate vision, sing only certain songs, abstain from alcohol, give up tobacco, not dance" and so much more. What a strange way to portray the apostle Paul's conviction: "It is for freedom that Christ has set us free" (Galatians 5:1).

These rules, regulations, expectations, and demands creep into our everyday conversation with persistent regularity. They betray a stronger view of God as judge than father, and such language eventually overwhelms many of us.

On the other hand, the Father image—especially as we see Jesus present it in Luke 15—shines the spotlight on grace. The law motivates us externally with guilt. Grace motivates us internally, from a heart overwhelmed by love.[8]

Security in the Father's Love

Henri Nouwen observed that we frequently spend our lives in pursuit of the security that comes only from being the beloved of God. In a classic article entitled "From Solitude to Community to Ministry,"[9] he suggested that many Christian leaders enter into ministry to gain prominence and acceptance in the community and thereby feel satisfied and secure in their private moments. For Nouwen, this completely reverses the biblical order that we see in the life of Christ and the apostles. Authentic ministry is not the pathway to security but the result of it. The apostles' absolute confidence in the love of God, first, allowed them to give rather than take and thereby genuinely enter into community with others. Ministry emerged naturally from those connections and relationships. Whenever we reverse the biblical model, we can expect counterfeit results.

> *Authentic ministry is not the pathway to security but the result of it.*

We could diagram the two paths as follows:

Model A

Ministry → Community → Security

Model B

Security → Community → Ministry

I've been teaching church leaders and pastors in college and university settings since 1994. Over the years I've met some leaders (both paid and volunteer) who lead *out of* their security but many others who lead *to find* security. Anyone who needs to lead for the affirmation it offers, the power it affords, or the prestige that accompanies it has not settled the issue of security.

Jerry pastored a small rural congregation of eighty members. As their shepherd, he felt obliged to manage everything that happened. He wanted veto power on the board and made it clear that new ideas should be presented to him for approval. Congregational members ought not to start new ministries without his knowledge and oversight, and the part-time youth minister quickly learned that he needed to give full and complete account for every choice he made and program he planned.

Jerry modeled major control issues in his life. He depended heavily on his title as pastor and his power as shepherd to feel secure, and as he guided the flock, albeit with a heavy hand and a stifling oversight, he formed a vague sense of self-importance and value. Jerry lived under Model A.

Of course, Model A also applies to many who are not pastors or church staff members. We may all fall into it as we seek to micromanage or control our families, workplaces, or volunteer ministries. Anytime we seek affirmation through our performance, we live under Model A.

We may exhibit our insecurity through inflexibility, competitiveness, defensiveness, and self-promotion. On the other hand, authentic security gives birth to the opposite traits: humility, cooperation, facilitation, and supporting others. False security depends on skills, abilities, personality, or charm. But true security doesn't arise from our parents or our culture. The security that empowers us to be servant-leaders has to do with our being the beloved of our Father. Have we discovered the Lord as our loving Father or do we serve Him as the landlord who demands an account of our efforts?

The first reference to the Holy Spirit the apostle Paul makes in his epistle to the Romans declares, "The love of God has been poured out within our hearts through the Holy Spirit who was given to us" (Romans 5:5 NASB). Did you notice? While we look for spiritual gifts, power, anointing, skills, and wisdom, Paul declares that the most vital role of the Spirit is to convince us of God's love and pour that love into us. Perhaps that's why Paul would later pray for the Ephesians that they might be able "together with all the saints, to grasp how wide and long and high and deep is the love of Christ, and to know this love that surpasses knowledge [and thereby] be filled to the measure of all the fullness of God" (Ephesians 3:18–19).

Jesus' Own Security

Even the ministry of Jesus was launched from this same foundation of the Father's love. When Jesus arose from His

Jordan baptism, He heard the Father declare, "This is my Son, *whom I love;* with him I am well pleased" (Matthew 3:17).

Jesus' ministry does not begin with educational how-to courses or words of advice for dealing with stubborn people and conflict. It begins with a powerful affirmation of His belovedness, which gives Him the strength and conviction to face testing in the wilderness and ultimately the horrors of the cross. The love of the Father sustained Him through the rejection and opposition He encountered during His ministry.

In another strategic moment in Jesus' life, we find the Father reiterating that love. Matthew records a pivotal moment in Jesus' journey toward Golgotha. In Matthew 16, Jesus asks His disciples, "Who do people say the Son of Man is?" (v. 13) and "Who do you say I am?" (v. 15). The disciples tell Jesus the rumors and speculation that they've heard, and Peter bursts out, "You are the Christ, the Son of the living God" (v. 16). Then Matthew tells us:

> From that time on Jesus began to explain to his disciples that
> he must go to Jerusalem and suffer many things at the hands
> of the elders, chief priests and teachers of the law, and that
> he must be killed and on the third day be raised to life (v. 21).

What a critical turning point in the ministry of Jesus. Up to this moment, He has taught the multitudes, performed miracles, and enjoyed a widespread popularity among the peasant class. But He now turns His face toward the cross, and the whole issue of identity and security arises once more.

In this context, Matthew tells us that after just six days Jesus took Peter and James and John with Him up onto a high mountain. Suddenly Moses and Elijah appeared to them, talking with Jesus. Peter is stunned and immediately offers to build special memorials for all three in that obviously sacred spot. But the purpose of the visitation is not to build monuments but to deliver a familiar message. The voice of the Father spoke from the clouds: "This is my Son, *whom I love;* with him I am well pleased. Listen to him!" (Matthew 17:5). The baptismal statement that marked the commencement of Jesus' ministry is repeated to mark the commencement of Jesus' journey toward the cross.

What did Jesus need to hear from the Father? Not "Everything will be fine. Trust me," but "I love you." His courage and obedience emerged not from fear but from being loved. Indeed, it is love—more than any other trait—that defines the Father.

Fear and Love

We constantly make decisions motivated by fear. In fact, the world trains us to be afraid and to use fear to control each other. Little wonder then that when we

> *When we live in the house of fear, we live superficially.*

have opportunity to lead people (our children, our colleagues, our churches), fear rises as the default mechanism and we find ourselves either intimidating others or feeling intimidated by them.

Many of us fear losing our status or position, fear negative comments, fear being thought incompetent or weak or, worst of all, fear failure. Is there a worse way to describe our parenting, our jobs, our ministries, or ourselves than as failures?

Fear isolates us and typically produces one of two responses from us. On the one hand, it may paralyze us and make us incapable of action—frozen with fear. On the other hand, it may push us to achieve more than ever before—a fear-driven frenzy. In other words, it produces extremes. The common denominator, however, is the outcome. When we live in the house of fear, we live superficially.

The skeletons in our closets terrify us. Anxiety about the future grips us. We grow consumed with the need to preserve our carefully cultivated facades. Cracks in any of this could kill us, or so we think. So we work hard to build emotional fortresses to protect ourselves and calm our fears. We construct a hard veneer and withdraw within the shell.

In contrast, the apostle John declares that "perfect love casts out fear" (1 John 4:18 NASB), and throughout the Bible we keep bumping into the divine admonition: "Do not be afraid!" (e.g., Joshua 1:9 NKJV; Matthew 1:20). We might take the hint that there's another more meaningful and deeply enriching way to live. But too few people find this better way.

That way is love—a deep, abiding, life-changing experience of the love of the Father. His love shines forgiving light into the dark closets of our lives. His love is unrelated to our performance and thus disconnects us from our achievements or failures. His love guarantees a secure future. His love alone delivers us from the house of fear. And each time we utter the word *Father* in the Prayer, that name opens the door of our fear and insecurity and invites us outside to freedom.

When fear afflicts us, we find freedom in faith. But such faith rests not on our ability to please the Father but the assurance that the Father's pleasure has nothing to do with our performance, and this assurance sustains us, even as it sustained Christ.

Our own journey through life turns a strategic corner when we no longer feel the need to pursue the approval of others but can rest assured in the love of the Father. Our preoccupation with what others think of us and how others assess us can create compulsiveness within us. Shalom (peace and holistic well-being) flows not from the opinions of our peers but the affirmation of the Father. When we hear Him whisper into our souls, "You are my beloved child," we can finally begin to shake off the striving and obsession that drives us, and often His whisper to us comes in response to our whisper to Him—*Father.* No longer is He the cosmic cop or the harsh landlord. "Abba! Father!" calls us His beloved children.

In the Family

Father. The parental term oozes unexpected intimacy. Something less familiar feels more appropriate (perhaps *God* or *Holy Divine One*), but the gospel calls us to a family reunion, not a meeting with the CEO. Truly good news restores intimacy to lives dried out by detachment. Is there a more gospel word than *Father*?

Our Father. The combination of the two terms binds us together as family and refuses to validate private faith. It acknowledges the new community—a family—to which we now belong.

Matt and Tami headed to Ukraine, in the summer of 2007, to find and adopt a new son. Their six-week trip included travel, interviews, paper work, and tough decisions. But that young boy, a complete stranger to the Armstrongs in June, became a member of the family in August. He would thereafter use the terms "Dad" and "Mom," and those titles would speak of acceptance, belonging, love, and protection. Matt and Tami did not sign him up for a mere club membership. He joined a family.

> *Is there a more gospel word than* Father?

Likewise, when we use the term *Father,* we find that our focus rests not only on God himself but also on those around us, the family into which we've been born again. To speak of His fatherhood is also to speak of our brotherhood. Robert Banks observed, "Paul's application of *household* or *family* terminology has all too often been overlooked or only mentioned in passing [but] the comparison of the Christian community with a *family* must be regarded as the most significant metaphorical usage of all."[10]

Evangelical Christianity has tended to preoccupy itself with viewing the church as the body of Christ, where everyone has a role to play and every role is important. But this image often deteriorates into something impersonal and mechanistic. It reduces the church to a factory or assembly line where each person fulfills their role, does their job, or exercises their ministry gift. In contrast, the image of family that the Prayer implicitly promotes calls us to a much more relational way of life. The priority and purpose of the church is not a task but people.

> *The priority and purpose of the church is not a task but people.*

When Jesus said, "Pray in this way," He disturbed the comfortable solitude of spiritual elitism. Christ refused to endorse any pursuit of holiness or godliness that does not include community. He anathematized individualism. *Our Father* snaps us out of complacency, privatism, and segregation. The words tumble forth with warmth, invitation, connection, closeness, security, love, and family.

Our faith finds its footing in *our Father*—an inch of lettering that bridges our seclusion from each other and the Lord. It declares good news and reorders the foundations of our lives—lives now lived in the context of love and family; lives now marked by security and companionship; lives now devoted to grace and mutual support.

CHAPTER 3

=======In the Heavens =======

Developing a Cosmic Perspective

St. Augustine wrote *The City of God* following the fall of Rome in AD 410. In it he attempted to console the shell-shocked Romans, who could hardly believe the defeat they had suffered at the hands of the Visigoths. Augustine insisted that if they would keep their eyes fixed on heaven, eventually the mystical, heavenly city of God would triumph over earthly politics. He encouraged them to deal with the disillusionment of the moment by looking beyond the visible; advice that has found numerous adherents throughout Christian history.

Under the bonds of slavery, African-Americans wrote and sang spirituals in the eighteenth and nineteenth centuries. Songs like "Swing Low, Sweet Chariot" did more than while away time during stiflingly hot days in tobacco fields or sticky evenings on a porch. These spirituals reflected a hope based in a heavenly perspective. Such songs, while connected to ancient biblical stories—in this case the story of Elijah's miraculous ascent into heaven—bore testimony to a greater reality that awaited; the heavenly reality that no amount of slavery or mistreatment could diminish.

> Swing low, sweet chariot,
> Coming for to carry me home,
> Swing low, sweet chariot,
> Coming for to carry me home.
> I looked over Jordan, and what did I see?
> Coming for to carry me home,
> A band of angels coming after me,
> Coming for to carry me home.

Our vision of the heavenly realm—even the throne room of God—can sustain us through the most difficult of days and circumstances. It births hope amidst hardship and nurtures faith amidst opposition.

Biblical Exhortations and Examples

The writer to the Hebrews wrote: "Let us fix our eyes on Jesus, the author and perfecter of our faith, who for the joy set before him endured the cross, scorning its shame, and sat down at the right hand of the throne of God. Consider him who endured such opposition from sinful men, so that you will not grow weary and lose heart" (Hebrews 12:2–3). Let us *fix our eyes* on Him, *look* at Him, and *see* Him. The fact that Jesus no longer walks in bodily form among His disciples does not deter the writer from inviting us to see the unseen.

Similarly, the apostle Paul wrote, "Our struggle is not against flesh and blood, but against the rulers, against the authorities, against the powers of this dark world and against the spiritual forces of evil in the heavenly realms" (Ephesians 6:12). He urges us to be alert to the greater reality that accompanies the visible realm. Behind what we see exist multiple layers of struggle in the heavenlies.

Both writers used language that calls us to a different perspective, to set our focus in a different place. Importantly, this shift of focus does not mean simply anticipating a future time when circumstances might be different. Instead, the language relates to a different reality that exists right now. We ought not to think that the heavenlies (or even heaven) lie beyond the grave. Rather, they lie just beyond our natural vision, and sometimes men and women this side of the veil have been privileged to glimpse some of their glory and wonder.

Elisha's servant rushed in with grim news. The Aramean army had come to get Elisha and dispose of him. That morning the servant stepped casually outside the door (perhaps to collect some water or the morning paper), and he saw the advancing army completely surrounding the city of Dothan in which he and Elisha lived. What to do?

In a panic, the servant cried out to Elisha, "What shall we do?" (2 Kings 6:15). Elisha prayed a simple prayer: " 'O LORD, open his eyes so he may see.' Then the LORD opened the servant's eyes, and he looked and saw the hills full of horses and chariots of fire all around Elisha" (2 Kings 6:17). The threatening circumstances had completely distracted the servant. Then in an act of grace the Lord opened the frightened servant's eyes to see the angelic hosts that stood between the city and the advancing armies. That cosmic perspective—recognizing the greater reality that lay behind the apparent circumstances—dramatically changed the servant's attitude, and the rest of the story.

Just four or five decades later the great prophet Isaiah also received a life-changing glimpse behind the veil:

> In the year that King Uzziah died, I saw the Lord seated
> on a throne, high and exalted, and the train of his robe
> filled the temple. Above him were seraphs, each with six
> wings: With two wings they covered their faces, with
> two they covered their feet, and with two they were fly-
> ing. And they were calling to one another: "Holy, holy,
> holy is the LORD Almighty; the whole earth is full of his
> glory."

Isaiah 6:1–3

Did you notice that Isaiah connects the throne of God with the Temple in Jerusalem, and it's the whole *earth* that is to be filled with His glory? In Isaiah's vision, God does not dwell in a remote, far-off celestial zone. Instead, Isaiah's eyes were opened to see a reality behind the visible reality.

Our Father *in the Heavens*

As we have seen, the opening words and phrases of the Lord's Prayer set the tone for everything that follows. *Our* calls us into community. *Father* invites us into intimacy. Now the phrase *in the heavens* adds to the foundation. It challenges us to adopt a cosmic perspective, to acknowledge the spiritual realm amidst our physical realities. As Willimon and Hauerwas note, "This thing between us and Jesus is not merely personal; it's cosmic."[1]

Jesus literally says, "Our Father *in the heavens,*" not the shorter *"in heaven"* that we commonly learn. Unfortunately, many believers who memorize the short version naturally assume that it refers to God's distance from us. After all, heaven (as we understand it) comes after death, so it's a long way away both in time and space. However, Jesus never intended that we view our Christian lives in terms of "us here" and "Him there," or "Him *way out* there!" We need to approach the phrase "in the heavens" differently. As we grasp the cosmic worldview that Jesus hints at in this simple phrase, we find ourselves much better prepared for living out the rest of the Prayer. Without understanding the simultaneity of the physical and spiritual realms, we find ourselves mired in a superficial (and somewhat defeated) faith. Spiritual maturity involves a growing awareness of the unseen world and its interplay with the material world in which we live.

Thomas Kelly, an early twentieth-century Quaker, wrote:

Between the two levels [of the seen and the unseen] is fruitful interplay, but ever the accent must be upon the deeper level, where the soul ever dwells in the Presence of the Holy One. For the religious man is forever bringing all affairs of the first level down into the Light, holding them there in the Presence, re-seeing them and the whole world of men and things in a new and overturning way, and responding to them in spontaneous, incisive, and simple ways of love and faith. Facts remain facts, when brought into the Presence in the deeper level, but their value, their significance, is wholly realigned.[2]

Jesus' simple little phrase *in the heavens* opens up a strategic dimension to our spiritual formation and discipleship.

The Jewish View of the Heavens

In the English language, the word *heavens* typically refers to the vast expanse of outer space, the stars, and galaxies that dot the night sky millions of light-years away, the planets and comets, the supernovas and black holes, the universe. These heavens extend way beyond our grasp and our visual abilities. We marvel at the photographs sent back by the Hubble Telescope and the staggering images of beauty that the Jet Propulsion Laboratory make available.[3] Does Jesus want us to pray to the Father who created and inhabits these remote regions? Yes. However, in Jewish cosmology of the first century, the *heavens* incorporated multiple layers.

The air around us that we breathe, and that birds fly in, forms the *first heaven*. The vast expanse of the night sky constitutes the *second heaven*. The spiritual, nonmaterial throne room of God—beyond the visible and the material—is the *third heaven*. You may recall the apostle Paul wrote of being caught up into this third heaven (2 Corinthians 12:2) where he saw a vision.[4]

Thus, when Jesus teaches His disciples to pray, "Our Father *in the heavens,*" and uses the plural form of *heaven,* He intends us to see at least two aspects of the Father: (a) His nearness—as near as our very own breath, and (b) His enormity—not confined to our small world but truly Sovereign of all creation. To the Jewish hearer, the plural term *heavens* would immediately evoke both thoughts. Jesus did not say, "Our Father in the third heaven," which would have made sense to Jewish listeners, but would also have highlighted the Father's remoteness or inaccessibility. Instead, Jesus uses *heavens,* and by doing so He casts a vision for a much more comprehensive perspective of the cosmos. As the psalmist noted:

> Where can I go from your Spirit?
> Where can I flee from your presence?
> If I go up to the heavens, you are there;
> if I make my bed in the depths, you are there.
> If I rise on the wings of the dawn,
> if I settle on the far side of the sea,
> even there your hand will guide me,
> your right hand will hold me fast.

Psalm 139:7–10

Matthew's Use of Heaven

Scholars have long wondered about the phrase *kingdom of the heavens,* which we find throughout Matthew's gospel.[5] In fact, Matthew uses the phrase thirty-two times and is the only New Testament writer to use it. Some have concluded that "kingdom of the heavens" (preferred by Matthew) and "kingdom of God" (preferred by the other Gospel writers) have the same meaning and that Matthew chooses the term *heavens* as a substitute for the term *God* out of sensitivity to his Jewish audience's reluctance to use the name of God.[6] However, this seems unlikely.

First, although Matthew prefers the phrase *kingdom of the heavens,* he also uses the phrase *kingdom of God.* If he intended to protect the sensibilities of his readers, he violates those sensibilities on four occasions (12:28; 19:24; 21:31, 43).

Second, as Dallas Willard notes, "It is certainly true that the word *heaven* is often used in the Bible to refer to God's realm— though I think never, strictly speaking, to God himself."[7] The Jews had (and have) no difficulty using the word *God* or *Lord* or other titles. While they steered away from pronunciation of the personal name of God revealed to Moses in Exodus 3:14—*YHWH*—they often spoke the generic name of *God.* Indeed, Matthew shows no special sensitivity to the name *God* in the forty-six other instances throughout his gospel where he uses it.[8] The gospel writer might easily have written about the *kingdom of the Lord* without offending his readers. But he didn't. He repeatedly used the term *kingdom of the heavens.*

It seems that when Matthew uses the term *heavens* he has something quite specific in mind.[9] And in the Prayer, Jesus describes the Father as the one "in the heavens."[10] The phrase clearly carries a special importance that we don't want to miss.

The Transcendence of God

First of all, *in the heavens* refers to the transcendence of God. He inhabits the vast heavens of the night sky as well as the hidden heavens of the spiritual realm. He transcends our own limitations. Clearly, He far exceeds the stone, wood, and bronze idols of the first century—figurines made by human hands. Furthermore, as the One in the heavens, He has power over any regional pagan deities or demons.

In a day when our familiarity with God has bred something dangerously close to contempt—that is, an overemphasis on the nearness (and friendliness) of God—we might restore some respect for His transcendence.

We tend to view the Father in very casual terms. The translation of *Abba* (Romans 8:15; Galatians 4:6) as "Daddy" and the emphasis on His approachability and openness to intimacy can undermine reverence and awe, or what the Bible calls "the fear of God."[11] We might still feel fear, but the kind usually born out of guilt or shame or anxiety about judgment, not awe at the character and glory of the Father. Perhaps too often we reduce the Sovereign God to "our best buddy." Has our familiarity with God clouded our assessment of His majesty and glory?

> *Has our familiarity with God clouded our assessment of His majesty and glory?*

The phrase *Father in the heavens* certainly nudges us back toward a deep sense of our limitations and His boundlessness, our finite lives and His infinite existence, our shortsightedness and His all-knowing. Thus, *in the heavens* guides us away from over-familiarity and can restore reverence. It seems as though Jesus complements the closeness of God (by using the intimate term *Father*) with the transcendence of God (*in the heavens*).

Ancient Israel dared not touch the mountain of the Lord (Mount Sinai—Exodus 19:12) because they feared His wrath and destruction. They dared not even try to look upon Him, knowing that His glory would utterly overwhelm them. We have few such reservations.

However, contemptuous familiarity with the divine hardly posed the major problem in Jesus' day or with Jesus' original Jewish audience. Consequently, it seems far more likely that Jesus intended those first hearers to hear the phrase with a different emphasis.

The Nearness of God

We've just seen that *in the heavens* reinforces the transcendence of God, but it also speaks of His nearness because the first heaven is the very air we breathe. He comes as near to us as the air in our lungs. We "live and move and have our being" (Acts 17:28) in His very presence. Just when we think of Him as remote, we discover that He dwells beside and within us. When we understand the nuances of *in the heavens,* we realize that the phrase speaks of both God's superiority over and above us and His incredible closeness to us.

Throughout Christian history, various godly men and women have written much about practicing the presence of God. By that they mean living each moment fully aware of His nearness and fully aware of His greatness. Herein lies a basic element of our spiritual formation.

His presence without our awe produces a sappy familiarity on our part. Our awe without His presence results in a meaningless and lonely spiritual quest. Neither leaves us satisfied or fulfilled.

Practicing His Presence

Strangely enough, *in the heavens* calls us back to practicing the presence of God in this moment and in this place. The spiritual aimlessness and powerlessness that many of us experience suggests that we need revitalization in this area.

Too often we maintain orthodox doctrine, mainstream beliefs, and traditional biblical teachings, but our faith remains strangely hollow. Have we reduced the power of Christ to the predictability of principles? The presence of God can too easily become a theological deduction rather than a personal experience. A.W. Tozer wrote,

The presence of God is the central fact of Christianity. . . . The type of Christianity which happens now to be the vogue knows this Presence only in theory. It fails to stress the Christian's privilege of present realization. According to its teachings we are in the presence of God positionally, and nothing is said about the need to experience that Presence actually. . . . For the most part, we bother ourselves very little about the absence of personal experience.[12]

Tozer cuts close to the bone. Perhaps we sometimes fail to experience the presence of God because we grow preoccupied with life itself or with what we are doing for Him. The busyness of our days, the fullness of our schedules, the absence of silence and solitude, our refusal to rest, the constant clamor of voices, the incessant emails, voice mails, and text messages, all conspire together to block our hearing of Him and distract us from walking with Him. Like Adam, we cease walking with Him in the cool of the evening and find ourselves a lifestyle that refers to Him but barely needs Him. Under such circumstances, the Father becomes our absent landlord—treated reverentially, spoken of respectfully, obeyed periodically, but distant and unknown. We perceive His presence to be in the third heaven rather than all the heavens.

> *Have we reduced the power of Christ to the predictability of principles?*

Do we find ourselves proclaiming a system of belief rather than the tangible presence and authority of the risen Christ in the world? We correctly affirm the Bible as God's Word but treat it like a last will and testament that God produced before

His departure. We respect it and read it and do what we can to apply it, often without much expectation that He is intimately present to speak through it. Even more, we may doubt that He has any current word for us except through this printed page.

Tozer's comments challenge our status quo, just as Jesus' prayer challenged the status quo of His first-century hearers. The Jews enjoyed a privileged position as the people of God, while at the same time failing to experience the dynamic and personal presence of the Father in each of their lives.

One of the most renowned writings on this topic emerged from the seventeenth century. Brother Lawrence, as we know him, provided the content for a short book entitled *The Practice of the Presence of God,* in which he described the wonderful joy of sharing his life in the monastery kitchen with "the Lord of the pots and pans."

In the twentieth century, Frank Laubach—a missionary to the Philippines—discussed in his journal an experiment that changed his life. "I resolved that I would succeed better this year with my experiment of filling every minute full of the thought of God than I succeeded last year. And I added another resolve—to be as wide open toward people and their need as I am toward God."[13] That attitude is truly living with God *in the heavens*: fully aware of God and fully aware of what He is doing in the lives of those around us.

Practicing the presence of God proves life-changing for anyone who dives into it. However, we cannot practice the presence of the Father very effectively when we live by distraction.

Living by Distraction

Spiritual ADHD (Attention Deficit Hyperactivity Disorder) runs rampant among us. More and more of us seem unable to be still, to focus, to wait, or to listen. We fill our lives with more and more "stuff" that has less and less significance. A tragedy or crisis may stop us briefly. But then it passes.

We hurry from appointment to phone call to email—or from school to shopping to sport—living by distraction. We prefer the pace and the demands because they lull us into a feeling of importance. Busy people are important people. Who wants to visit a doctor who is on time and has no line of patients in the waiting room? The delays affirm their importance—an importance we'd all like. Conveniently, the pace we embrace also drowns out the voices of Christ and others who might point out the thin ice we live on.

> *Spiritual ADHD runs rampant among us.*

Generally speaking, we're much more comfortable with busyness than stillness. We prefer constant noise to silence (just note the next church service you attend). We want to dismiss the quiet place as tedious or unproductive, but those labels simply mask the fact that we feel threatened by silence.

Barbara Brown Taylor concludes, "Sometimes I think we do all the talking because we are afraid God won't. Or, conversely, that God will."[14]

On the one hand, we'd like God to speak to us. But, if necessary, couldn't He leave a voice mail or email that we can check when it's convenient? We're open to His guiding our lives, but we'd be happy if He'd just bless our dreams and plans. We'll follow Him anywhere, at the appropriate season of life. We want to be obedient, but then hurry along lest He actually issue an instruction.

Perhaps the central challenge of our day is not to find *time* for Christ but to find the *courage* to stop for Him. Contrary to popular claims, the distractions of our lives do not emerge from the world. We create them and empower them. We choose to carry the cell phone, turn on the computer, load up the iPod, work early and late, and arrange "business lunches." Our schedules, despite our complaints of "a life out of control," remain largely under our control. We make choices every hour.

> *Perhaps the central challenge of our day is not to find* time *for Christ but to find the* courage *to stop for Him.*

Our choice to live by distraction undermines our intimacy with each other and with the Father. The distractions become destructive when they clutter our lives, plug our ears, and blind our eyes to spiritual realities. It's hard to see the cosmos while we're distracted. Yet despite the struggles, Jesus invites us to encounter the Father who inhabits both the seen and unseen heavens. The Prayer reminds us that every place we go and every experience we have falls under His watchful gaze. We may distract ourselves from Him for a lifetime, but He is never distracted from us. We may defer giving Him our attention, but He remains constantly attentive to us.

In the heavens describes more than just a place (or places). It affirms the Father's focus on us. More than that, it reminds us that we run the race in the presence of *many* witnesses.

Never Alone

In the mid-1990s, I visited the village areas outside Chennai, India. The sights, sounds, and smells left a deep impression. But the real surprise—everywhere, at every hour of the day and night, I saw people. Laborers slowly placed pavers on a city street at 2 a.m. Men and women walked in the rural fields in the light and the dark. The roads seemed constantly noisy and busy, especially with huge trucks belching out clouds of black exhaust. Open spaces began to produce claustrophobia.

My experience in India reflects a spiritual reality, too. Everywhere we go, the saints surround us. Sometimes they have flesh and blood like us, most times not. Our entire lives are immersed in the company of the "called." Those in Christ who have died before us have not abandoned us through death. Instead, they have joined the cloud of witnesses who continue to observe us:

> Therefore, since we are surrounded by such a great cloud of witnesses, let us throw off everything that hinders and the sin that so easily entangles, and let us run with perseverance the race marked out for us.

Hebrews 12:1

It seems that the gathering of past saints into eternal bliss does not separate them from us. On the contrary, those saints and family across the bar form the cheerleading squad urging us to run with endurance the race that is set before us.

The presence of Christ is awesome, but this crowd of onlookers is also wondrous. Should we pray to these people or seek to reconnect with them? No. The writer to Hebrews urges us to "fix our eyes on Jesus." The Father, Son, and Holy Spirit are our track companions. But we do not run the race unnoticed by earlier contestants. Indeed, we honor them by learning from their journeys and remaining faithful to our calling.

This invisible crowd envelops us. We live in community and find constant company even when we sit seemingly alone.

Those who have passed from this life to the next remain surprisingly near to us. They sit in the stands, with bated breath, watching, and perhaps cheering. They anticipate that glorious day when the races all finish and the celebrations begin for all God's people, together.

Heavenly Minded

"Too heavenly minded to be of any earthly use!" That charge sits uncomfortably with most of us and to guard against it we may stop looking too deep or too far. But from Jesus' perspective, if we drop our eyes below the horizon we sacrifice a foundational feature of our faith.

C. S. Lewis countered the accusation of heavenly-mindedness when he wrote: "Aim at heaven and you will get earth thrown in. Aim at earth and you get neither."[15] On another occasion he stated: "If you read history you will find that the Christians who did most for the present world were precisely those who thought most of the next. It is since Christians have largely ceased to think of the other world that they have become so ineffective in this."[16]

In a similar vein, David Shibley has written:

Remember a "heavenly minded" Wilberforce whose passion for human dignity helped eradicate the slave trade throughout the British empire. . . . Scan the world and look at the thousands of hospitals, shelters, leprosariums, children's homes, and colleges that have been built in heaven's honor. The point is obvious. Those who truly set their sights on another world are often the most active for constructive change in this one.[17]

In the heavens. As we pray this short phrase it speaks equally of the Father's majestic throne room and His amazing closeness—as close as our own breath. The apostle Paul wrote, "Praise be to the God and Father of our Lord Jesus Christ, who has blessed us in the heavenly realms with every spiritual blessing in Christ"

> *God blesses us in every realm at every time, because of Christ.*

(Ephesians 1:3). His words remind us of Jesus' Prayer. God does not restrain His blessings for the hereafter or some Peter

Pan Neverland. He blesses us in every realm at every time, because of Christ.

In the heavens. The phrase beckons us to a greater cosmic perspective than ever before.

CHAPTER 4

— Hallowed Be Your Name —

Pressing Toward Holiness

Hallowed be your name.

The English word *profane* originates in the ancient world. *Profanus,* in Latin, referred to the area literally "before or outside the temple." By contrast, the ancient Romans identified the temple area itself as the *sacrum,* the sacred place.[1] Initially, therefore, profane pointed to a place, but these days it describes an attitude we might have, an attitude of irreverence or disregard for God. It stands in total contrast to the sacred and the holy.

Symptoms of an increasingly profane world abound. In one study of U.S. television programming between 1998 and 2002, cursing rose 95 percent during the television family hour—eight to nine each evening. The very next hour showed a 109 percent increase.[2] This dramatic rise in irreverent language, profanity, and cursing reveals the heart of our culture. But just as disturbingly, it also shapes the heart of our culture. Much as contaminated water flows from a polluted source and poisons us, so these words spill forth from corrupt hearts with their destructive consequences. As we listen to them, we grow increasingly desensitized to them, and they mold us.

Symptoms of an increasingly profane world abound.

Frankly, in a profane world, holiness seems archaic or quaint at best, a Puritan ideal, a relic from medieval monasticism, or a sign of naïveté.

When police found the lifeless body of thirty-nine-year-old Anna Nicole Smith in the Seminole Hard Rock Hotel in Florida in February 2006, American television and cable companies considered it big news. This aspiring Marilyn Monroe, famous for her immorality and profane lifestyle, occupied national headlines for weeks. As best we can tell, she made no meaningful contribution to society and did nothing in the areas of philanthropy, social activism, or compassionate service. Her celebrity status arose from her poses for *Playboy* magazine and her marriage to the aged oil tycoon J. Howard Marshall—sixty-three years older than her. Yet her story captivated the media and our culture.

Similarly, when Paris Hilton, the twenty-six-year-old socialite and heiress of the Hilton family fortune, spent twenty-two days in jail, in June 2007, for driving on a suspended license (following an earlier conviction for drunk driving) the courtroom and jailhouse saga received headline attention in the print media, on television, and on the Web for weeks. Hilton's only claim to fame was her wealth and notoriously loose lifestyle, but millions of people tuned in for daily updates on her life.

We live in a time when the lewd, crude, immoral, and profane receive center stage not because of our disgust or shame but because of our fascination.

We may not want to return to the shaming silence of the Victorian era or the draconian days of Prohibition, but our moral standards are in disarray. We have relaxed our censorship expectations such that graphic material that once received mature audience ratings now filters regularly into PG-13 movies, deemed generally acceptable for preteens. While society maintains laws about illicit drug use, we tend to ignore prescription addictions or "soft" narcotics for personal and recreational use.

The list continues endlessly. We've seen dramatic downgrades in fashion standards, music lyrics, radio commentary, dating behavior, and online etiquette. In every area of our lives, obscenity, indecency, and profanity prevail. From the hallways of the high school to the cubicles of the corporate world, secularism has secured its place, and sin flaunts itself.

None of us can live on an island isolated from these influences. Unless we turn off the television, refuse the newspapers, avoid the Internet, return our iPhones, and stay indoors in our own homes, we will face this stark reality. We cannot avoid it. And every living generation must deal with it.

Under such circumstances, holiness looks very old-world. Surely it belongs to a simpler, less complex time. Yet when Jesus laid out the Prayer, He urged His disciples to pray, "Hallowed be your name."

The Prayer has already established the centrality of community (*Our*), the primacy of love (*Father*), and the importance of seeing beyond the visible (*in the heavens*). Now Jesus expands His teaching by identifying the principles and values that will guide His disciples into genuine fullness of life. Once we agree to pursue community with each other, intimacy with the Father, and awareness of the spiritual—the basic prerequisites for any meaningful life journey—we then need instruction on the practical steps in such a journey. The first step, according to Jesus, has to do with holiness—God's holiness; but to exalt His holiness requires a commitment to holiness on our own part. We cannot hallow His name without also considering hallowed lives of our own. *Hallowed be your name.*

The Jewish Holiness Tradition

The Jewish audience that first heard Jesus utter the Greek word *hagiastheto* ("hallowed"—"made holy") surely connected the word with their long holiness tradition as a nation.

In Leviticus 11:44, the Lord declared to Israel, "Be holy, for I am holy" (NASB). This mandate summarized the goal of all the moral, judicial, and ceremonial laws prescribed throughout the book of Leviticus. It applied initially to the priesthood. However, the priests served as representatives of the entire nation and the Lord intended that Israel would one day become a "kingdom of priests"[3] where every person lived out holiness in both of its basic aspects—set apart for the purposes of God and living lives of purity and wholeness. The Israelites would then accomplish God's plan and live with others in redeemed and perfect relationships. That day still awaits us.

For the early church, the word *hallowed* signified "to make a person or thing the opposite of *koinos,* common."[4] In the New Testament, *hallowed* describes the gold on the temple (Matthew 23:17), the consecration of the Son by the Father (John 10:36), and the setting apart of the believer for God (Acts 20:32). In fact, a common designation of all believers is "saints" (literally, "sanctified ones" or "holy ones").

The Jewish holiness tradition, first expressed through Moses, and earnestly pursued by the Pharisees,[5] is actually completed by the saints—every person who chooses earnestly and sincerely to follow Christ. What began in the Sinai Peninsula with Jewish refugees from Egypt finds fulfillment ultimately among all God's people in eternity.[6] We as Christians carry that torch right now, and the Prayer calls us to it.

Two Approaches

We can approach "hallowed be your name" from two perspectives.

First, it simply expresses a fact. God's name, which represents His character and person, is wholly separate from us. In other words, "Lord, you sure are different from us!" Names in the Bible often do much more than simply identify someone or something. They describe something of the character of a person or communicate an insight about a person. The name change of Abram ("exalted father") to Abraham ("father of a multitude"—see Genesis 17:5 NASB) provided a reminder of God's remarkable promises every time someone called out the new name. Similarly, when Jacob ("one who takes what belongs to someone else") became Israel ("He who strives with God"—see Genesis 32:28 NASB) an entire story came to mind. We could mention others, too, but the name Jesus itself represents the pinnacle of purposeful naming: "You are to give him the name Jesus, because he will save his people from their sins" (Matthew 1:21).[7] Consequently, to set apart the name of God involves acknowledging His otherness, His greatness, His power, and His character.

However, "hallowed be your name" also carries a second and much richer connotation: "Lord, may you be honored by the way we live." In essence, we declare our desire and intent to live differently. The idea of hallowing is closely linked to the notion of glorifying, and when we say that we *glorify* the Father, the term means that we "show forth His charac-

We declare our desire and intent to live differently.

ter," not just announce it. In the same way, we "hallow" the name of the Lord not only with words of adoration but with lives of obedience and surrender. And we pray that He might be honored by our lives.

We see this connection between behavior and reputation every day that we watch the news. When police arrest a teenager for lewd conduct or criminal behavior, our minds unavoidably make some assessment of the teenager's parents. The "family name" is brought into disrepute by the unacceptable actions. Similarly, we hallow or besmirch the name of the Lord by our lifestyles.

Hallowed be your name.

The Profane First Century

We tend to view ourselves as unique. We think that nobody has ever faced the issues that we face, and we regularly assert that the world has never been more complex than it is right now. We point to an electronic and digital world with information exploding exponentially through the Web. We itemize the extraordinarily complex ethical issues that societies have not had to address in the past.[8] But we err if we think, even for a moment, that Jesus did not understand the forces and power of secularism. We display our ignorance if we suggest that Jesus did not encounter the profane and the vulgar.

First-century Israel did not resemble a pleasant garden party. The extreme poverty, whereby the average lifespan of men and women was about forty years and half the babies born did not make it to their fifth birthday,[9] created vacuums of hopelessness, fear, and desperation. Without a Social Security system to support widows and orphans, they became potential victims of unscrupulous men, forced (at times) into immoral and degrading living arrangements.

While ancient Israel recognized the reality of *YHWH,* the common people (the "sinners" as the Pharisees liked to label them) were bent on survival. They lacked our iPods and iTunes, email and voice mail, Web sites and satellite stations, but they shared the same basic subsistence needs: food, shelter, security, and love. The toys have changed dramatically, but the foundational needs of humanity have not changed a bit. We might contrast their primitive lifestyles with our sophisticated lives, but such a contrast has little relevance. The human heart, tempted by pride, greed, lust, and fear, remains sadly consistent across the centuries.

Thus, when Jesus invited His followers to pray, "Hallowed be your name," the word *hallowed* (or the more familiar *holy*) would surely have struck a dissonant chord with them then, just as it does with us today. Isn't holiness the privileged prerogative of comfortable and affluent people with the time and resources to pursue godliness? Can the poor and the suffering really strive for holiness when they need to focus all their energy and attention on survival?

Reluctant Holiness

In our own day, holiness seems such an abstract concept, and Christ's call for us to embrace it causes considerable confusion and inner-conflict. We might speculate at least a couple of reasons for this phenomenon.

The challenge of swimming upstream usually intimidates and overwhelms us.

First, holiness sounds like a lifestyle out of touch with our cultural reality. We use phrases like *party pooper, prude,* or *conservative* to marginalize people who don't join the mainstream hurtling toward the falls. And the challenge of swimming upstream usually intimidates and over-whelms us. Holiness definitely sounds like against-the-stream kind of living in an age of widespread irreverence.

As my eighteen-year-old son approached his high school graduation, his circle of friends planned a calendar full of events and outings. Few of them had curfews imposed by their parents. A co-ed overnighter seemed perfectly acceptable to everyone. As we talked together about the conflict of standards—the standards of the secular school environment and the standards of the kingdom of God—Matthew spoke the words that we've all wanted to express at one point or another: "It's just so hard! I'm always the one who doesn't, can't, or won't. It's just so hard!"

Absolutely. When Christ calls us to live in such a way as to bring honor to God, He knows full well that such a choice has a high price tag attached to it. He called it "taking up our cross to follow Him" (see Matthew 10:38), "dying to ourselves" (see Matthew 16:25), and "counting the cost" (see Luke 14:27–28). We cannot worship God and serve Christ while also living for ourselves and following the secular crowd.

We also hesitate to embrace holiness in our day because it smacks of exclusivity and judgmentalism in a culture where nothing is sacred. People battling their own hurts, habits, and hang-ups, hardly delight in self-righteous religious fanatics who ooze criticism and condemnation. Holier-than-thou-ness seriously taints any enthusiasm to pursue genuine holiness.

Too many believers distinguish themselves by their fin-ger-pointing, name-calling, and labeling of others. While we want to name sin for what it is, we also want to guard against judgmentalism. The hypocrisy of some saints has left others of us a little gun-shy. Of course, such stereotyping emanates from both sides of the divide. For example, as pro-life picketers call abortion-rights activists "baby-killers," the pro-choice activists retort with hurtful labels of their own, and the conflict becomes framed in judgmental language. No one wants to speak of holiness in such contexts. It seems to fuel the conflict.

> *If Christian spirituality neglects the pursuit of holiness, it fails entirely.*

However, if Christian spirituality neglects the pursuit of holiness, it fails entirely. We cannot dismiss the pursuit of holiness on the grounds that it is unpopular or might be misinterpreted. As the writer to the Hebrews noted, "Make every effort to live in peace with all men and to be holy; without holiness no one will see the Lord" (Hebrews 12:14).

A Necessary Hypocrisy

Have you ever been accused of hypocrisy? Most of us hate that label, but in some ways such an accusation confirms our significance to society.

People who fail to aspire to any standard higher than what they already live out pose a genuine risk to society. When our fallen condition becomes the acceptable benchmark, we plateau with grave consequences.

Imagine if we simply caved in to violence. We recognize conflict as a normal part of human life. But if we decided that assault was inevitable and therefore made it acceptable, the downward spiral would be swift and dramatic. Similarly, if we decided to abolish laws about sexual harrassment or indecency, what kind of work environment might develop? Civilization has always depended upon our legislating to a higher standard than we sometimes observe.

Nevertheless, we generally reserve our strongest criticism for those who advocate a high standard but fall short of it in practice. When a person's words and deeds don't align perfectly, we do not hesitate to label them as duplicitous, two-faced, double-standard hypocrites. We expect their actions to match their words. The irony in all of this glares at us. Can we be human without hypocrisy at times? Can we hope to elevate society to high levels of civilization if we only advocate standards we never violate? Of course not. Our failure to model full and utter integrity does not render integrity a pointless or unnecessary pursuit.

Unfortunately, our hasty and harsh judgment against hypocrisy breeds a deep spiritual problem. When we feel that we must avoid hypocrisy at all costs, we inevitably live false lives, deceiving both ourselves and others.

On the one hand, we deceive *others* about the truth and reality of our lives. We create a facade to hide our flaws and failures, since we dare not look hypocritical. We specialize in "image management"—our image—and toil endlessly to convince others that we are something other than what we are.

On the other hand, and perhaps more sinister, we deceive *ourselves*. The apostle John wrote, "If we say that we have no sin, we deceive ourselves, and the truth is not in us" (1 John 1:8 KJV). To avoid the charge of hypocrisy we project to others only our best side and, with time, we grow to believe our own press and justify or deny our "minor" indiscretions.

> *Those whose standards are only as high as their lifestyles never change society.*

If we see our own sinfulness and have the courage to acknowledge our own failures and at the same time advocate the higher standards of the kingdom, we cannot avoid hypocrisy as the world defines it. The gap actually affirms our commitment to Christ and the transforming journey of faith.

To see our sinfulness and *not* affirm a higher goal is to wallow in darkness and deny the life-changing potential of the kingdom and the Gospel. Our silence about holiness either consigns us to hopelessness or drives us to spiritual arrogance.

Perhaps when onlookers accuse us of hypocrisy, we might accept it more as a backhanded compliment than a hurtful criticism. Those whose standards are only as high as their lifestyles never change society.

Yes, we must grieve the gap between our ideals and our reality, but never settle for the deception of utter consistency in a fallen world. Ours is a necessary hypocrisy.

The Fathers

The holiness tradition within the church has a long and unbroken trail of advocates. Over the centuries, men and women have steadfastly insisted that the Christian life reflect the holiness (virtue) of Christ. Listen to just a few of those voices.

Gregory of Nyssa, a fourth-century church leader sometimes described as the "Father of Mysticism,"[10] observed in his own day that "just as the end of life is the beginning of death, so also stopping in the race of virtue marks the beginning of the race of evil."[11]

Thomas à Kempis lived in the fifteenth century. His classic work, entitled *The Imitation of Christ,* has been one of the most widely read and recommended books in all of Christian history. In it, Thomas à Kempis addresses the inner life of the believer but also insists on the moral and ethical responsibilities of Christian discipleship with exhortations such as "Learn to stamp out your vices, for this will serve you better than knowing the answers to a whole list of hard questions."[12]

William Law, a devout Anglican priest of the eighteenth century, admonished his hearers, "It is as great an absurdity to suppose holy prayers and divine petitions without a holiness of life suitable to them as to suppose a holy and divine life without prayers."[13] He could not imagine that people would pray earnestly without giving attention to their life choices and the pursuit of holiness.

We focus on the details of our lives precisely because we long to see the name of the Father "hallowed." We honor Him in the eyes of others as we show forth His character consistently and comprehensively. The old saying "The apple doesn't fall far from the tree" implies that a son's character (expressed in his behavior) probably gives us a fair indication of his father's character. What does our lifestyle declare about God? If we intend to glorify the Father by the way we live, then His standards must increasingly become ours. The apostle Paul noted, "You were bought at a price. Therefore honor God with your body" (1 Corinthians 6:20). This commitment to die to ourselves and press hard after God certainly challenges our "whatever" mentality.

The "Whatever" Generation

Armchair sociologists call us the "whatever" generation. It's not a technical term, but an accurate one. Whatever you want; whatever suits you; whatever you think. We may disagree, but . . . whatever. I may have hurt you, but . . . whatever.

This laid-back approach to life produces indifference ("I don't care") and indolence ("I'm not going to do anything about it"). But the consequences run much deeper. Like a seeping appendix, it poisons us and abandons the holiness of the Father.

"Whatever" grows out of relativism—that rampant philosophy that defies biblical moral absolutes. In its simplest form, relativism insists that what is true for you is well and good, but don't force your standards (or your interpretation of God's standards) on me. As long as we act sincerely and with tolerance toward each other . . . whatever. But this insipid mindset, so prevalent among us, has a high cost.

When we abandon a common standard (God's) and let each person determine their own ethical standards, the inevitable outcome is chaos. The book of Judges finishes with the sad line: "In those days Israel had no king; everyone did as he saw fit" (Judges 21:25). Israel seemed trapped in a cycle of oppression and hardship because they, like us, had a "whatever" attitude. But beyond the chaos and conflict, consider for a moment a more soul-destroying outcome.

> *Only absolutes can evoke authentic absolution and genuine grace.*

Only absolutes can evoke authentic absolution and genuine grace. No absolutes; no forgiveness; no grace. Let me illustrate.

Karen and Jeff got into a terrible argument. Jeff had lied to her about a paycheck that he had gambled away on his way home from work. Their marriage was a roller-coaster at the best of times, but this event took them to a new low. She felt deeply hurt that Jeff had squandered hard-earned money when they had bills to pay. But she was most outraged that he had lied to her when she confronted him. For her, responsibility and integrity had "absolute" written all over them. For Jeff, the whole incident was little more than a "whatever." He couldn't understand all the fuss. Consequently—and follow this—any apology from Jeff would lack sincerity (another violation of integrity!) and any forgiveness offered by Karen would be relatively meaningless to Jeff. If he's done nothing terribly wrong, there's nothing to be terribly sorry about, and nothing to be terribly forgiven for. He just wants their argument to blow over and their lives to settle back down. Jeff can experience neither forgiveness nor grace while he fails to share the absolute values that Karen holds. He'll no doubt regret stirring up the hornet's nest, but that's a different matter altogether.

If we hold different standards of right and wrong (ethics) then true forgiveness cannot be given or received. We wallow in pain and shame, and our culture offers just one word of consolation: *whatever.* It fails entirely to heal, reconcile, redeem, or restore. Instead, it exacerbates our isolation and despair. The veneer of freedom in our culture—whereby we can do basically *whatever* we like—only enslaves us. True freedom does not mean lack of restraint. Just the opposite. Authentic freedom comes from the decision to live within godly boundaries ("Hallowed be your name") and forgive those who violate those boundaries. We cannot dismiss or modify those standards, but grace allows the fallen to return. In contrast, *whatever* casts us adrift, without moorings and without hope.

The cultural arm-wrestle between absolute ethics and *whatever* ethics has grace implications. The irony is obvious. Relativism, which looks like it gives everyone their own freedom, begets bondage. Absolutes—the holiness of the Father—lead to life.

The Father always seems distant and remote to those who fail to see their own sin. Such people deny their need for grace, mercy, forgiveness, or renewal, though in quiet moments of reflection they experience deep tides of dissatisfaction with their lives. In contrast, John Newton—the eighteenth-century slave-ship captain—could write of amazing grace because its light shone into the darkness of his own life and drew him to the holiness of God. No *whatever* for him.

Without awareness of our sin and guilt, we cannot enter salvation and grace as fully as the Father desires. Thus, grace emerges from the absolute standards mirrored in His holiness, not the feeble *whatever* philosophy of our times. The Lord's statutes spring from His character and do more than simply sustain society. His principles pave the path to grace and life for each of us.

His Holiness and Our Fulfillment

Unless our desire for the Divine recognizes and responds to His holiness, we simply create a god in our own image with which we superficially console our deepest yearnings. Such a god deceives and betrays us, leaving us self-absorbed, self-justified, and increasingly self-deluded.

The holiness of our Father delivers us from misguided mysticism.

In hallowing His name we acknowledge that His holiness enables our fulfillment. *Our Father,* when isolated from holiness, degenerates into fair-weather and frothy friendship. Without holiness, we assess His fatherliness in purely human terms and the outcome invariably reduces Him to an acceptable version of ourselves.

His holiness lifts us beyond the mire of our human experience, if we dare pursue such genuine liberation. His holiness highlights the shortsightedness of secularism, the poverty of profanity, and the futility of immorality. When we hallow His name, he confronts everything destructive and poisonous within us.

His holiness refuses to ignore our *un*holiness. Perhaps therein lies the explanation for our reluctance to pray this phrase with our hearts. While our lips mouth the words, our hearts hesitate at the implications and potential costs.

His holiness refuses to ignore our unholiness.

We cannot yearn for His holiness to pervade the world—and our inner world—and simultaneously be complacent about our current condition. Indeed, what we declare of Him He desires for us, precisely.

Hallowed be your name.

CHAPTER 5

Your Kingdom Come

Overturning Our Kingdoms

Your kingdom come.

Alexander the Great bemoaned: "Do you not think it a matter worthy of lamentation that when there is such a vast multitude of [worlds], we have not yet conquered one?"[1] The young Greek King, who died just short of his thirty-third birthday three centuries before the birth of Jesus, enjoyed unprecedented power in the ancient world. In less than ten years, he successfully spread the Greek language, culture, religion, and political ideals around the Mediterranean and across the Middle East. Yet he felt anguished by his slow pace in conquering other kingdoms.

History repeatedly reinforces that human kingdoms rise and fall with regularity. Pharaohs, Caesars, kings, emperors, czars, presidents, prime ministers, queens, chieftains, and dictators have come and gone with metronomic rhythm. They have often ruled with great economic and military power, control-ling nations and even empires—but only for a season.

Jesus' Kingdom Message

According to the Gospel writers, Jesus came preaching a simple message: "The time has come. . . . The kingdom of God is near. Repent and believe the good news!" (Mark 1:15). But the kingdom that He announced transcends geographical and temporal limits. His kingdom would not be measured in terms of mountains and seas or decades and centuries. And those who heard Jesus use the phrase *kingdom of God* knew full well that this proclamation surpassed the ambitious longings of a Babylonian Nebuchadnezzar, a Persian Darius, a Greek Alex-ander, a Syrian Antiochus, an Egyptian Ptolemy, or a Roman Caesar. The words, though spoken by a Nazarene peasant, carried power and re-ignited a dream that had begun to fade among the first-century Jews.

If we had lived in first-century Palestine, this kingdom language would have struck a deep, resonating chord within us. Israel's history included numerous setbacks. Everyone recalled the glorious years of King David a thousand years earlier, when he significantly expanded the kingdom of Israel. Under his reign, Israel controlled more territory than ever before or ever since. But his son and successor, Solomon, could not maintain the grip. Following Solomon's disappointing reign—about 925 BC—the nation divided into a northern kingdom (Israel) and a southern kingdom (Judah).

From that day on, Israel experienced cycles of division, displacement, and exile. The Assyrians conquered the northern kingdom in 721 BC, and the Babylonians defeated the southern kingdom in 586 BC. Then the Persians, the Greeks, the Syrians, the Egyptians, and finally the Romans, all dominated Israel in the 350 years before Christ.

Now Jesus arrives with a startling message: "The kingdom of God is near." If this didn't create a buzz, nothing would. To the Jewish mind, the kingdom of Israel *was* the kingdom of God. Consequently, this word from Jesus bore revolutionary overtones. No wonder, then, that at one point the people planned to make Him king by force (see John 6:15). They could not wait any longer. This message aroused their crushed hopes and fueled their flagging hearts. They felt ready for revolt and uprising. They could almost taste the end of nearly a thousand years of conflict and suppression. Jesus was about to restore the kingdom.

> *The Prayer challenges us to pursue God's kingdom rather than our own.*

After His resurrection, as Jesus gathered with His disciples, they asked the obvious question:

> "Lord, are you at this time going to restore the kingdom to Israel?" He said to them: "It is not for you to know the times or dates the Father has set by his own authority. But you will receive power when the Holy Spirit comes on you; and you will be my witnesses in Jerusalem, and in all Judea and Samaria, and to the ends of the earth."

> Acts 1:6–8

Jesus had certainly primed the pump. Kingdom expectations ran high. Even in the Prayer, He taught His disciples to pray, "Your kingdom come. . . ." Every time they prayed this prayer, their focus would return to the kingdom of God—not that it was ever far from their minds. The Prayer would further inflame their kingdom longing. But Jesus had something else in mind. His contemporaries looked around and grew bitter at the Roman oppression. They yearned for liberation. They ached for the restoration of Israel, for the return of their land, for God's people to gain preeminence among the nations, for God's favor. But the Prayer challenged them to adopt a new kingdom mentality, to pursue God's kingdom rather than their own.

Just when we want to say, "Our kingdom come, with your help and blessing," Jesus redefines the focus. He will not sanction any kingdom but the Father's, despite the fact that the Lord created us to reign.

Created to Reign

When God created the heavens and the earth, He gave us a special privilege.

Then God said, "Let us make man in our image, in our likeness, and *let them rule* over the fish of the sea and the birds of the air, over the livestock, over all the earth, and over all the creatures that move along the ground." So God created man in his own image, in the image of God he created him; male and female he created them. God blessed them and said to them, "Be fruitful and increase in number; *fill the earth and subdue it. Rule over* the fish of the sea and the birds of the air and over every living creature that moves on the ground."

Genesis 1:26–28

We typically associate the "image of God" with the characteristics of God—able to think, reason, communicate, love, laugh, and build community. But the context of this ancient Mosaic text suggests that to be made in God's image is to rule. "Let them rule over the fish of the sea and the birds of the air. . . . Fill the earth and subdue it. Rule over. . . ." In short, God designed us to enjoy dominion just as He does. He created us—in part—to rule, to reign, and to manage His creation. He wired us to exercise benevolent reign under His own sovereignty. Yet we distort this creation purpose. Instead of good and kind stewardship (implicit in the term "rule over") we exploit the earth. Furthermore, we extend our dominion to include people—a step beyond God's design and intention.[2] Consequently, we spend our lives either seeking to dominate other people or avoid domination by them. We have completely misunderstood this creation principle of dominion.

> *God has hardwired us for dominion.*

Nevertheless, this theme of our dominion courses its way throughout the Bible. Even in Revelation, John anticipated that our dominion would continue into eternity.

You have made them to be a kingdom and priests to serve our God, and *they will reign on the earth*.

Revelation 5:10

Blessed and holy are those who have part in the first resurrection. The second death has no power over them, but they will be priests of God and of Christ and *will reign with him* for a thousand years.

Revelation 20:6

There will be no more night. They will not need the light of a lamp or the light of the sun, for the Lord God will give them light. And *they will reign for ever and ever*.

Revelation 22:5

God has hardwired us for dominion and it will continue into eternity to the "new heaven and new earth" (Isaiah 65:17; 2 Peter 3:13) in its purest and most honorable expression.

In the sixteenth century, John Calvin remarked, "Everyone . . . carries a kingdom in his breast."[3] He meant it in less than flattering terms, but it reflects a solid (and good) biblical principle. Perhaps when we see two-year-old children begin to express possessiveness—"That's mine!"—we are not so much witnessing the emergence of their selfishness as the immature expression of their innate kingdom/dominion consciousness.

When our young child refuses to hand over control of his toy to a friend (or stranger), our parental tendency may be to gently scold and admonish him to share. We feel a little embarrassed by the display of selfishness, hoping that our model offspring might demonstrate a generous spirit rather than ugly self-centeredness. But if control of "stuff"—dominion—reflects the God image within us, we might expect that as soon as we're old enough to know that something belongs to us, we will want to control or manage it.

The dominion principle has significant implications in this discussion about kingdoms. As we begin to pray, "Your kingdom come," we immediately, perhaps unknowingly, invite His kingdom to take priority over our own. Such an invitation inevitably creates a tension and struggle within us.

His Kingdom and Our Kingdom

The essence of Christian spirituality revolves around participation in our Father's kingdom, not retreat into our own.

We typically spend our lives seeking to expand our own kingdoms—increasing our assets, resources, and influence. Our kingdoms can include the workplace, the church, the club, the sporting team, and the home, and we grow very protective of anything into which we have invested our time, energy, and money.

When people challenge our kingdom, we react defensively and perhaps even with hostility. This simple observation of human nature makes Jesus' prayer all the more extraordinary: "Your kingdom come."

Any invitation for God's kingdom to come threatens our own kingdom. Kingdoms are, by definition, mutually exclusive. Any domain with two kings is ripe for conflict. Thus, we might express the phrase "Your kingdom come" another way: "My kingdom done!" The Lord's kingdom displaces our own.

What does this mean for our day-to-day experience? If we pray this phrase sincerely, it demands surrender of our values to embrace His; submission of our will to His; and the ceding of our ambition in favor of His. It means releasing into His hands the reins we hold so tightly.

"Your kingdom come" does not invite the Father to come and watch us, but to come and rule us. We do not invite Him to partner with our lives, but to take charge of them. This three-word phrase, recited by believers for the past two thousand years, beckons an enormous lifestyle upheaval, if we're serious.

God calls us to live in His kingdom. The Father does not seek opportunity to live in our kingdoms.

We may sometimes pursue God as a not-so-subtle way to expand our own dominion. We seek Him so that He'll grant us what we desire. Everybody wants a generous grandpa. But this simple prayer—when uttered with integrity—strips away such selfish intentions. Jesus reminds us that God calls us to live in *His* kingdom. The Father does not seek opportunity to live in *our* kingdoms. Thus, at the end of the Sermon on the Mount, in which Jesus embeds the Lord's Prayer, He adds, "Seek first his kingdom and his righteousness, and all these things will be given to you as well" (Matthew 6:33).

The End of Personal Ambition

Our culture values ambition. We honor men and women with ambition: go-getters with initiative, drive, energy, and vision. They know what they want and they chase it hard. They study and toil long hours driven by what they want to achieve. And generally speaking, we'd prefer our children to grow up with the same strong focus and direction. For most of us, apathy represents the opposite of ambition, and we sense that the progress of civilization—or even the progress of our family—is better served by drivenness than dormancy. Consequently, we ask questions like, "What do you want to do when you grow up?" and we encourage our children to strive for significance and success.

It's not that we expect them to become Alexander the Greats or Napoleons. Napoleon, short in stature, did not lack in ambition. His desire to conquer the known world (and thus expand his own kingdom) drove him even to the fatal mistake of attempting to invade Russia in winter—a mistake that Hitler repeated. Napoleon's pursuit of personal glory drove him to a coup that ultimately led to the Battle of Waterloo and his final defeat. His unchecked—and uncheckable—ambition overrode his wisdom and better judgment in strategic struggles. We certainly don't want our offspring to be destroyed by ambition, but we encourage a healthy dose of it.

When we open the Scriptures, we find that the New Testament authors present ambition, success, and drive in very different terms. *The New International Version* translates the

Greek word *eritheia* as "selfish ambition." It occurs in the following texts:

> . . . idolatry and witchcraft; hatred, discord, jealousy, fits of rage, *selfish ambition,* dissensions, factions. . . .
>
> Galatians 5:20

> [Some people] preach Christ out of *selfish ambition,* not sincerely, supposing that they can stir up trouble for me while I am in chains.
>
> Philippians 1:17

> Do nothing out of *selfish ambition* or vain conceit, but in humility consider others better than yourselves.
>
> Philippians 2:3

> But if you harbor bitter envy and *selfish ambition* in your hearts, do not boast about it or deny the truth.
>
> James 3:14

> For where you have envy and *selfish ambition,* there you find disorder and every evil practice.
>
> James 3:16

In contrast, Paul uses another word for ambition, *philotimouo,* in just two places.

> It has always been my *ambition* to preach the gospel where Christ was not known, so that I would not be building on someone else's foundation.
>
> Romans 15:20

Make it your *ambition* to lead a quiet life, to mind your own business and to work with your hands, just as we told you.

1 Thessalonians 4:11

These two sets of verses highlight something fairly simple. Selfish ambition leads to chaos; godly ambition eliminates our pursuit of personal glory. The apostle Paul writes the quintessential text on godly ambition when he describes the burning desire of his heart in these terms.

> *Godly ambition eliminates our pursuit of personal glory.*

I consider everything a loss compared to the surpassing greatness of knowing Christ Jesus my Lord, for whose sake I have lost all things. I consider them rubbish, *that I may gain Christ* and *be found in him.* . . . *I want to know Christ* and the power of his resurrection and the fellowship of sharing in his sufferings, becoming like him in his death, and so, somehow, to attain to the resurrection from the dead.

Philippians 3:8–11

To pray, "Your kingdom come" provides another way to say, "I want to know Christ Jesus my Lord. Above all else, I want to gain Christ and know Him." It requires that we lay down our own agenda, our own ambition, and our own dominion. Such a prayer has dramatic implications. It silences self-promotion and guides us to more humble service.

The Discipline of Secrecy

In the verses surrounding Matthew's rendition of the Prayer, couched within the Sermon on the Mount, Jesus delivers a series of jolts to the religious tendencies of His day—and ours.

Religious living often deteriorates into false piety. Our best intentions to act righteously, to give generously, to pray faithfully, and perhaps even to fast regularly can quickly degenerate into exercises of self-promotion and self-glorification. What begins with a desire to "know Christ" or to call forth His kingdom, may transition into spiritual disciplines that draw attention to ourselves and stealthily expand our own kingdoms.

People admire those who give great sums or fast for long periods. So Jesus warns His disciples that *anything* we do to draw attention to ourselves—whatever we do before men *to be noticed by them* (see Matthew 6:1)—negates any reward from our Father in heaven. By contrast, the Father promises to repay us for any honorable and praiseworthy deed that we do in secret.

> When you give to the needy, do not let your left hand know what your right hand is doing, so that your giving may be in secret. *Then your Father, who sees what is done in secret, will reward you.*
>
> Matthew 6:3–4

> When you pray, do not be like the hypocrites, for they love to pray standing in the synagogues and on the street corners to be seen by men. I tell you the truth, they have received their reward in full. But when you pray, go into your room,

close the door and pray to your Father, who is unseen. *Then your Father, who sees what is done in secret, will reward you.*

Matthew 6:5–6

When you fast, put oil on your head and wash your face, so that it will not be obvious to men that you are fasting, but only to your Father, who is unseen; *and your Father, who sees what is done in secret, will reward you.*

Matthew 6:17–18

We frequently hear about the spiritual disciplines as strategic practices for spiritual formation. Prayer and Scripture, fasting and worship, giving and studying, silence and solitude. But what about secrecy? Have we considered the discipline of secrecy? Jesus urged His disciples not to let their left hand know what their right hand is doing (Matthew 6:3). In other words, their actions should not result from a careful calculation of the marketing value they might hold, but reflect obedience and humility before God.[4]

> *Have we considered the discipline of secrecy?*

When Jon Bon Jovi appeared on Oprah Winfrey's popular daytime television program in the first week of 2006, he presented a check for $1 million toward hurricane relief, the largest donation ever received on Oprah's show to that point.[5] That generous act overwhelmed the audience. But at the same time, Bon Jovi was promoting his musical albums. Did the check come from his marketing budget or from his heart? The public generosity made it very hard to tell.

We should delineate between secrecy over sin and this spiritual discipline of secrecy. Sin already encourages secrecy and finds power in it. When *Dateline NBC* set a sting for online sexual predators and then filmed men coming to the home of an underage girl, it became very apparent that those men, for the most part, lived horrifying double lives. Rabbis, pastors, lawyers, doctors, tradesmen, and others all fell into the net— but not by accident. They had been fishing. It cost many of them their marriages and did irreparable harm to their families. That kind of secrecy steals, kills, and destroys everything that the Father intends for us (see John 10:10).

On the other hand, Jesus advocates a different kind of secrecy. He encourages secrecy over acts of righteousness— those acts that lead us not into shame but potentially into pride. This version of secrecy has few advocates in our self-honoring culture.

We drop hints about our spiritual efforts or spiritual progress. We mention how sacrificially we serve, or quietly tell someone that we played a significant role in someone else's life. If we witness to a neighbor or assist the poor, we find ways to let others know about it.

Our culture teaches us to build a résumé, and we do the same with our faith. We casually drop names of "important" Christian figures we've met or worked with, Christian organizations that we've served, or churches where we've held official positions. We tell stories of our spiritual conquests and achievements, victories, and good deeds. But a fine line exists between the transparent selfless sharing of our lives to encourage others and proud self-elevation to enhance our own reputation.

We cannot practice the discipline of righteous secrecy if we need the accolades and recognition of people. Insecurity always drives us to have one better story than the next person. Our need for the approval of others—especially other Christians—may motivate us to great acts of sacrifice and service. But if we tell of those acts, we have (in Jesus' words) already received our reward.

> *We cannot build our private empires and His eternal kingdom at the same time.*

The discipline of secrecy prohibits the building of any spiritual résumé. It restrains us when we want to compare ourselves with the next person. It denies us the opportunity to advance our own standing in the eyes of the world. Any of us who would pray, "Your kingdom come" must consider this discipline with utmost seriousness. If the coming of His kingdom means the lessening of our kingdom, then we must strategically refuse to establish our own fame or renown. We cannot build our private empires and His eternal kingdom at the same time. "Your kingdom come" challenges the *silo thinking* that so often prevails among believers.

Beyond Silo Thinking

The silo metaphor is drawn from the grain silos that dot the rural landscape of Midwest America; they stand side by side, with very little connection to each other. Thus, the business world uses the phrase *silo thinking* to suggest that each department in an organization often functions as a silo and stands alone, not interacting with any of the other departmental silos.[6] Such isolation does little to further the cause of the business.

In the same way, many of our efforts for the kingdom of God can become personal attempts to actually establish and protect our own turf. Folk leave churches all the time because they feel thwarted in efforts to "build their own ministry."

Terry felt certain that God had given him a prophetic ministry. His earnestness in prayer—and private delight at having a "special" ministry to the body of Christ—made him increasingly persistent with his advice to the leadership at his local church. Over time, as the leaders of that congregation expressed reluctance to embrace all of Terry's advice, he accused them of resisting God. Before long, he had moved on to another church, where he hoped to get a more responsive reception.

Janine attended First Community Church, where she oversaw the women's ministry. In that small congregation, the women's ministry included small-group Bible studies, an annual retreat, and oversight of the kitchen area. When the church board offered $10,000 for a kitchen upgrade, they never anticipated the heartache, hurt, and division that such generosity would produce. Janine suddenly found herself at odds with several other women, each of whom felt protective about the kitchen as "their turf."

Silo thinking means building our own mini-kingdoms. It happens to us so easily that it can slip beneath our radar. Our first inkling of it may be a competitive feeling about someone else's "success" or a defensive reaction to any perceived "threat" to our own area of responsibility. "Your kingdom come" always helps defuse such thinking.

Throughout church history, division has more typically arisen from silo thinking than doctrinal differences. We hurt each other most when we grasp for our rights or fear loss of what we have built. The church at ancient Corinth experienced this kind of silo thinking. Some said, "I am of Paul." Others claimed, "I am of Apollos." And still others aligned themselves with Cephas or Christ (see 1 Corinthians 1:12; 3:4). Yet Paul counters their wayward thinking with this powerful reminder:

> What, after all, is Apollos? And what is Paul? Only servants, through whom you came to believe—as the Lord has assigned to each his task. I planted the seed, Apollos watered it, but God made it grow. So neither he who plants nor he who waters is anything, but only God, who makes things grow. The man who plants and the man who waters have one purpose, and each will be rewarded according to his own labor. *For we are God's fellow workers; you are God's field, God's building.*
>
> 1 Corinthians 3:5–9

Paul's punch line in verse nine puts it all in perspective. We do not work *for* ourselves or *by* ourselves. Instead, we serve as God's fellow workers, tending *His* field and building, not our own. Consequently, we hold loosely to our achievements and allegiances. In essence, Paul reminds the Corinthians to pray, "Your kingdom come." Later he would urge the Philippian believers to have the same attitude that Christ had, emptying themselves and considering each other as more important than themselves (see Philippians 2:3, 7). This forms the real crux of the prayerful statement, "Your kingdom come."

We do not work for ourselves or by ourselves.

As we pray, "Your kingdom come"—and understand some of its implications—it forces us to loosen our grip on our own kingdoms. It challenges our own selfish ambitions and prideful behaviors. It also confronts our competitive spirit and need for personal achievement. The Prayer, in this short phrase, inverts everything that we have considered normal and redirects our hearts toward the rule of God.

CHAPTER 6

══ Your Will Be Done on ══ Earth As It Is in Heaven

Transforming Willfulness to Willingness

Your will be done.

The two-year-old thrives within me, despite the intervening decades. At first, I learned some basic motor skills that let me control *things.* I discovered I could hold and drop objects at will. Before long I learned other skills (tantrums and strong-willed defiance) that let me control *people.* I got my way (often) and I've enjoyed the feeling ever since.

I'm much more subtle these days. No crying fits and much less pouting. I don't make nearly as many scenes in shopping centers, and I rarely stomp my feet. My wife won't tolerate it. But the two-year-old is alive and well within me—and possibly within you, too.

Willfulness—wanting and demanding that our will be done—reflects our fallenness. And the implications for our lives, and especially our spiritual journey, run deep.

When Jesus prayed in the garden of Gethsemane, "…yet not my will, but yours be done" (Luke 22:42), it sounded like the words of defeat. "All is lost. I can't get my way; so I guess you win." Instead, Jesus simply reiterated the theme of His entire life, words that open the door to real vitality. His life, contrary to ours, modeled this truth constantly.

In the Lord's Prayer, Jesus taught His disciples to pray, "Your will be done on earth as it is in heaven"[1] (Matthew 6:10). If spoken from the heart, and sustained as our life's guidepost, such a prayer will prove revolutionary. Nothing about our lives can remain the same when we speak these words sincerely. So we should be warned: The journey from "my will" to "your will" is no Sunday-afternoon stroll.

Our willfulness expresses itself in so many ways—anger when people threaten or thwart our plans, manipulation of others to get what we want, and competitive-

> *Willfulness reflects our fallenness.*

ness. Ironically, even high levels of self-discipline can indicate willfulness, unless we harness it to build relationships. The two-year-old rules us until we surrender *everything* to the Father.

Of course, we may "surrender" simply as a means to get what we want but can't get any other way. Such false claims or deceptive affirmations can be subtle ways to succeed or even to tacitly manipulate God. But the surrender that finally causes us to grow up is unconditional surrender. It's the willingness (not willfulness) to lose *everything* (including reputation and status) because of love—His love. None of us surrenders anything willingly for a lesser motive. And herein perhaps lies the clue as to why we remain so determined and aggressive in life.

Our occasional prayer is "Your will be done," but our common desire is "My will be done." Those in Christian leadership may have the deepest reflecting to do at this point. Do we ultimately lead for Him or for ourselves? Is our drivenness and competitiveness a symptom of a surrendered life or our spiritual immaturity? We might only imagine the utter transformation that surrender would make in our lives.

Willingness and Willfulness

Without a doubt, both our deepest struggles and highest joys come from the human will.

On the one hand, we wrestle within ourselves when we lack the willpower to do what we feel we could or should do. Consider the habits, hang-ups, and addictions that we battle. We hate losing another round to alcohol, drugs, lust, or anger. Then we clash with others when their will differs from our own—in marriage, family, and the workplace. On the other hand, we experience enormous delight if our will aligns with someone else's. We love to experience authentic agreement. If you've ever nervously proposed marriage to someone who enthusiastically said yes, you know the richness of authentic agreement.

When we coerce or manipulate each other, conflict abounds. When we submit *willingly,* unity prevails. Nothing hurts us as deeply as feeling disempowered or overpowered, and nothing breeds deeper resentment than to have our will devalued or demeaned. We hate the workplace where a boss or co-worker belittles or abuses us. We resent the friendship where we feel pushed around or taken advantage of because we can't say no.

What I want matters.

My parents didn't teach me that. Nor did I learn it in school. It's simply part of being made in the glorious image of God. God created us with the capacity to make decisions. He blessed us with a will to exercise.

What shall I want?

With typical insight, the Lord's Prayer addresses this cornerstone of our lives. Jesus teaches His disciples to *choose* the *will* of the Father. He does not advocate fatalism or pessimism, as though Christian belief crushes our choice. To the contrary, Christ reminds us that faith—defined as trust and commitment—delights in the will of the Father.

"Your will be done" springs from confidence that God's will is both informed and ideal. He wants what's best for us.

Interestingly, the prayer has no qualifiers: "Your will be done in looking after me, but my will be done in finding a marriage partner, choosing a career, deciding about my money, and planning my future." Jesus omits these add-ons as He urges us to learn the art and joy of willing surrender.

Your will be done. In other words, "We want what you want, and we receive what you give."

When we assert our own will, with God or with each other, our *willfulness* leads to pain and division. John Calvin wrote, "It is very necessary for us to be restrained by some discipline from breaking into willfulness."[2] He understood, as we do, that our natural tendency leans toward willfulness—demanding our own way—and it takes an intentional effort to subdue it. Yet when we submit our will to the Lord's, our *willingness* unexpectedly gives birth to life. Can faith be faith without walking this pathway?

Our greatest grief arises from a self-guarded will. Paradoxically, joy comes with willing abandonment to the Father. Still we struggle to simply trust Him. Even as we pray, "Your will be done," we secretly desire clarity.

We Want Clarity

Our pursuit of clarity has become one of our greatest idolatries.

We may not gaze at crystal balls or study tarot cards, but many of us are just as eager to know the future as our unbelieving counterparts. We pray, and pray hard, that God will reveal His will, by which we mean that He'll give us a glimpse of the future and the best course of action in a given circumstance. We don't want to make a mistake. And in our hunger for a hint of what lies ahead we find ourselves walking by sight (clarity) and not by faith (trust).

The Scriptures applaud Abraham because he obeyed God and started traveling "even though he did not know where he was going" (Hebrews 11:8). Similarly, many others trusted God with their lives (and deaths) despite not receiving "what had been promised" (Hebrews 11:39). In short, these saints of the past had unwavering confidence in the character of God and His call on their lives, and simply trusted everything else to Him.

Brennan Manning tells the story of the brilliant ethicist John Kavanaugh, who went to work for three months at "the house of the dying" in Calcutta. He wanted to know how best to spend the rest of his life.[3]

On his first morning he met Mother Teresa, and she asked, "What can I do for you?" Kavanaugh asked her to pray for him. "And what do you want me to pray for?" she asked. He expressed the deepest desire of his heart. "Pray that I have clarity." She said firmly, "No, I will not do that." Kavanaugh was taken aback. Mother Teresa continued, *"Clarity is the last thing you are clinging to and must let go of."* When Kavanaugh commented that *she* always seemed to have the clarity he longed for, she laughed and said, "I have never had clarity; what I have always had is trust. So I will pray that you trust God."

So often we want clarity. "If I choose this school, how will it affect my future? If we get married, will it work out? If we move there, will it be okay? If I take that job, will I be happy?" We can easily come to idolize clarity. We think it will resolve our anxiety and guarantee our success. Like inside traders on the stock market, we want secret information that will protect us from a loss.

> *Our pursuit of clarity has become one of our greatest idolatries.*

In the midst of it all, Christ calls us simply to trust Him, with a ruthless trust.

As the crucifixion loomed, the disciples grew increasingly confused and anxious. They thought they had clarity about the kingdom, and they wanted confirmation. Jesus would oust the Romans and liberate the Jews into the glorious messianic age. Right? Surely the script did not include more persecution and death. But Jesus simply refocused them: "Don't be stressed about what lies ahead; trust God, and trust me" (see John 14:1).

As we pray, "Your will be done," we surrender our need for clarity. We don't need to know the details of the future. We entrust them to the Father. We cease clinging to the false notion that if we can see tomorrow we'll be able to steer better today. The Prayer challenges us to let the Father do the steering.

As we surrender our need for clarity, we also learn to discard our fantasies.

Discarding Our Fantasies

Fantasies rarely shape reality. More often, they simply frustrate it. When we fantasize, we idealize something. And we fantasize in almost every area of life—wealth, power, sex, marriage, children, and even church (to name but a few).

Some fantasies seem harmless enough and perhaps even noble. We imagine what a great marriage would be like, if only this or that could be changed. We dream about a more friendly or successful church, if only the leaders or the church members would change in some way. But therein lies the danger. We romanticize how things could be, and miss the grace of God in what is. Dietrich Bonhoeffer wrote:

Every human wish dream that is injected into the Christian community is a hindrance to genuine community and must be banished if genuine community is to survive. He who loves his dream of a community more than the Christian community itself becomes a destroyer of the latter, even though his personal intentions may be ever so honest and earnest and sacrificial.[4]

How easily we travel into the wishful world, and find that it produces a critical spirit. "A truly godly leader would . . . If only this worship service was . . . These people are just not . . . My marriage

The wishful world produces a critical spirit.

would be so much better if . . ." Our fantasies and idealism, rarely grounded in reality, serve only to fuel a fire of unholy discontent.

We imagine how other people could be, and when they fall short, we are bruising in our reaction. We love the fantasy, but not the people.

Of course, we don't want to dismiss the value of visionary leadership or pressing toward maturity. But a chasm exists between vision for where God wants to take us and the fantasy of how we'd like things to be. Some of us have formulated an idealism that no living person or real community could attain. This fantasy then breeds frustration, not motivation. Eventually, we climb over most of the fences and realize that the grass looks much the same. The problem lies in our perspective.

Bonhoeffer pulls no punches. How deeply do we love those who've been given to us? Or do we long more deeply for those who don't exist?

Our fantasies, though sometimes well-intentioned, do more harm than good. They blind us to grace in the present moment. They discourage and disillusion us. They undermine the "fellowship of the fallen" and isolate us from those given to us. Such fantasies harm our marriages, our children, our churches, and us.

How deeply do we love those who've been given to us? Or do we long more deeply for those who don't exist?

When Jesus taught about the final judgment, He told His disciples that if they cared for the hungry, the thirsty, the stranger, the naked, and the imprisoned, they cared for Him. "I tell you the truth, whatever you did for one of the least of these brothers of mine, you did for me" (Matthew 25:40). Do we fantasize about serving such outsiders?

Let's discard the seductive phantoms, the "perfect" people and places, before we damage the real gift that we already have.

As we pray, *Your will be done,* we affirm our desire for His purposes, not our fantasies. But this phrase of the Prayer also confronts our desire to make big plans for our own lives.

Big Plans

At some point, many or most of us bought in to the prominent cultural view that we need goals and plans to be happy.

We've all heard it—"If we fail to plan, we plan to fail"—and who wants to fail?

I've stopped making New Year's resolutions. I used to feel noble in setting goals for the next calendar year—lose ten pounds (or more, depending on how much I had enjoyed the Halloween candy, Thanksgiving turkey, and Christmas goodies), read ten more books, run more miles (which would help with resolution #1), pray more, and spend more time with my family. Those resolutions usually fizzled by the third week of January, but I felt the peer pressure to set them initially. Interestingly, nobody organizes parties for February 1 to check up on the status of those resolutions.

These annual resolutions, however, represent just the tip of the iceberg. Our culture honors those with BHAGs (Big Hairy Audacious Goals).[5] Consequently, we plan, strategize, and learn to cast vision. We set goals in every area of life—spiritual goals, educational goals, parenting goals, career goals, financial goals, and more. And when, or if, we achieve those goals, we barely stop to acknowledge it because we're already aiming higher and further.

Goals stretch out endlessly before us like the horizon. Our life-journey becomes so preoccupied with this elusive and ever-changing future that we often fail to experience the present in the full. We grow so focused on the *Not Yet* that we can't see the *Now*. But *Now*

> *We grow so focused on the* Not Yet *that we can't see the* Now.

is the moment of God's presence, His real gift to us, and all we have to hold with any certainty.

Our relentless grasp for tomorrow becomes tomorrow's grip on us. The prospect of a new day and a better way distracts us too often from the reality of "God with us" right now and His will for us in this very moment.

Living with Christ in the Now delivers us from the guilt of the past and the fear of the future. Jesus declared to His disciples, "Surely *I am* with you always, to the very end of the age" (Matthew 28:20). We would likely say, *"I will be* with you always . . ."* but Christ casts it in the present tense. Why? Because to live for one day from now, one week from now, or one year from now is not to live life to the full *right now*. James put it this way:

> Now listen, you who say, "Today or tomorrow we will go to this or that city, spend a year there, carry on business and make money." Why, you do not even know what will happen tomorrow. What is your life? You are a mist that appears for a little while and then vanishes. Instead, you ought to say, "If it is the Lord's will, we will live and do this or that." As it is, you boast and brag. All such boasting is evil.
>
> James 4:13–16

The movie *Peaceful Warrior*[6] tells the story of a wise old gas-station attendant who teaches a young Olympic hopeful to stop focusing on Olympic gold and live fully in the present.

Gradually Dan, the talented gymnast, learns "there is never nothing going on" and if he'll be attentive to the moment he'll live a much fuller life. While the movie is not explicitly Christian and Dan is never guided to seek Christ in the moment, this principle has powerful Christian roots.

Our interest in the will of God tends to spring more from curiosity or fear than devotion to Him. We think it would be helpful to get a glimpse of our lives five years from now. We certainly don't want to make a mistake that could cause us grief. "Lord, a little guidance, please?" But this preoccupation with the future, more than the will of God, may hurt us more than help us. Perhaps we will find deepest satisfaction not in second-guessing the future but living fully in this moment, this day. As we live in His presence, we live in His will.

As we live in His presence, we live in His will.

Is it wrong to make plans? Of course not. The entire biblical story details the grand plan of God to redeem each of us. But when the future undermines our capacity to live fully with Him in the present, we enter constant restlessness rather than peace. When tomorrow preoccupies our focus because we live for "the plan" rather than the moment, we find ourselves unsettled and rarely satisfied.

Your will be done. This single statement requires trust and contentment and becomes a door to greater freedom. It's not a statement of passive resignation but a strategic decision to become a different person.

We Are What We Want

Thomas Merton once wrote: "Your life is shaped by the end you live for. You are made in the image of what you desire."[7]

We may not always get what we want, but we will always become what we want.

As human beings, we differ substantially from the inanimate objects of our everyday world. Unlike our cars, furniture, and kitchen utensils, our lives are constantly morphing into new shapes. We are forever "becoming" and Merton's insight resonates as true. We become what we desire.

Our desires tend to be extremely diverse, and change with time. Early in life we desire marriage and children, then we long for financial success and security, or we want to own a home, or enjoy success as a leader. Whatever desire drives us most in a given season, determines the shape of our lives at that time. We are the ultimate chameleons. For example, the person who is consumed with desire for a marriage partner may make a range of related life choices—about online dating services, exercise, clothing, and entertainment. We may even become what we are not in order to get what we want. Or consider how our desire for success can impact our decisions, our time-management, and our families. Ultimately, whatever drives us the hardest shapes us the most. As each desire takes hold of us, we find ourselves transformed. The challenge before us is to distill those desires into a single one— the desire for God.

God created us with desires, especially the desire for Him. We may not have drilled down that deeply, but it's true. All other dominating desires reflect distorted ways by which we seek to complete what only He can fulfill.

The desire for intimacy with another person in marriage actually reflects our desire for intimacy with God, whether we know it or not. Our desire for respect from others can only be satisfied by the full acceptance we experience from the Father. The desire for achievement often emanates from our need for significance or security, both of which we find most perfectly in Christ.

Psalm 73 introduces the third book of the Psalms, and Asaph begins with the words, "Surely God is good to Israel, to those who are pure in heart" (v.1). Throughout the psalm, Asaph admits that he envied the arrogant when he saw their prosperity, and he cries out that the wicked are "always carefree, they increase in wealth" (v.12). Has he kept his heart pure in vain? Then he wakes up to himself and affirms that despite his own hardships in the moment, "Earth has nothing I desire besides you [Lord]" (v. 25b). Surely this defines what Asaph means by "pure in heart." Purity of heart is not primarily a moral issue but one of singular and preeminent desire for God.

Similarly, and much later, Jesus declares in the Sermon on the Mount, "Blessed are the pure in heart, for they will see God" (Matthew 5:8). Here, as in Psalm 73, the text may revolve less around moral purity and more around a single, unadulterated desire for God.

The apostle Paul models this same purity of heart when he gladly discards everything he has desired in the past to pursue wholeheartedly the one desire of his present—to know Christ Jesus. He writes, "I consider everything a loss compared to the surpassing greatness of knowing Christ Jesus my Lord, for whose sake I have lost all things. I consider them rubbish, that I may gain Christ" (Philippians 3:8).

We may not always *get* what we want, but we will always *become* what we want. Merton got it right. And as we pray, *Your will be done,* we develop a purity of heart, a singleness of focus that transforms us. This phrase is not just about who gets their way—us or God—but what we become. The journey from willfulness to willingness, however, calls for courage—the courage to surrender.

His Will—Our Passion

We usually think of *passion* as an emotion. But the Latin root of the word (*passus*) is the same root for our English word *passive*. The Old English use of the word *passion* referred to suffering—that which happened *to* a person, not what a person *did*.

In that light, Henri Nouwen writes:

> The great mystery of Jesus' life is that he fulfilled his mission not in action but in passion, not by what he did but by what was done to him, not by his own decision but by other people's decisions concerning him. It was when he was dying on the cross that he cried out, "It is fulfilled."[8]

Our culture, even our Christian subculture, generally takes a negative view of passivity. Christian men's movements demand that men reject passivity. Peers and pastors urge us to "seize the day, take the initiative, and just do it!" We glamorize the go-getters and those who "make it happen." In a performance-driven, power-hungry, action-oriented, competition-based culture, passivity is anathema. But such an attitude proves seriously toxic to our spiritual formation.

We have an important choice to make. We may surrender as an act of resignation—what will be, will be—or as a calculated decision to release control: Not my will, but yours be done. The first speaks of a defeated attitude, the latter demands genuine courage. We ought not to equate passivity with inactivity or apathy. To the contrary, it demonstrates the ultimate suppression of my own desires that I might fulfill His desires. While the apostle Paul wrote, "I die daily" (1 Corinthians 15:31 KJV), we would hardly describe him as inactive or apathetic—in his life or his ministry. Nevertheless, he understood himself as the vessel through whom the Father worked.[9] The daily death was a daily surrender to Christ of Paul's own ambition, drive, goals, dreams, expectations, desires, hopes, and vision.

Our passion for God cannot be defined by enthusiastic emotion, loud cries of praise, or fervent claims of allegiance, but by *the willingness to undergo anything to know Him more*—whether sickness, bankruptcy, persecution, or failure. These experiences may become our greatest allies in drawing us deeper into His presence.

Mary's gentle affirmation, "May it be done to me according to your word" (Luke 1:38 NASB) demonstrated genuine passion in the oldest sense of the word. It did not involve hype, ecstasy, or wild gyrations. It simply emanated from the will.

Cathy Davis suffered from an incurable degenerative disorder in her back. For twenty years she endured doctor's visits, medications, and limitations. In the last few years she found herself basically bedridden. One night in February 2006, while her husband traveled on business to Florida, Cathy watched Mel Gibson's movie *The Passion of The Christ*. As she saw the suffering of Jesus, she quietly prayed, "Lord, if you'd go through that for me, then I'm willing to endure this small affliction without complaint. However, if you see fit to heal me, that would be fine, too!" She could not have been more genuine or sincere in her sentiment of submission. Though she already walked closely with Christ, that evening she utterly surrendered her affliction to the Father. The next morning she awoke to a healing. Doctors who had described her as permanently disabled and beyond medical options marveled at her pain-free state. Cathy had received a miracle.

Unfortunately, we might focus too heavily on the miracle and presume that surrender of our will becomes the pathway to miracles. Not at all. Many others who have surrendered their wills to the Father have continued to endure hardship. The apostle Paul himself prayed three times that a certain "thorn in the flesh" might be removed from him, without "success."[10] But Cathy's quietly whispered prayer reminds us of Mary herself: "May it be done to me according to your word." Here we see true passion.

In leadership, people perceive "waiting" as weakness, view "releasing" as compromising, and confuse "surrender" with indecision. Consequently, we want to seize control decisively, set an agenda forcefully, and assert a vision aggressively. The world calls it passion, and will even applaud it. But somewhere along the line, as we begin to realize that the largest parts of our lives are not under our control, that we are not as independent or self-sufficient as we have claimed, the emotion can no longer carry us.

Perhaps then (and only then) we are ready to loosen our grip and let God take the initiative—to love us and work through us. "We know that in all things God works for the good of those who love him, who have been called according to his purpose" (Romans 8:28).

Ultimately, life is not what we make of it but what He makes of it.

The illusion of action reflects the fruit of a self-absorbed culture. As Nouwen briefly noted, "Passion is what finally determines the course of our life."[11] Ultimately, life is not what *we* make of it but what *He* makes of it.

May our passion for God produce increasing submission to Him so that He may do to us, through us, and with us whatever He wishes. Disciples of Jesus can do no less. *Your will be done.*

CHAPTER 7

Give Us This Day Our Daily Bread

Learning Dependence and Simplicity

Give us this day our daily bread.

Zimbabwe was mired deep in political and economic crisis in 2007. Analysts expected the annual inflation rate for the year to reach 100,000 percent.[1] Rocketing prices, exorbitant customs tax on any cross-border products, and an intransigent government, produced enormous shortfalls within the small African country.

Sidyne Mavozda, principal of the Zimbabwe Christian College, a school training pastors, sent a letter to friends and supporters that September. It read, in part:

I cannot remember the last time we had bread at the college. . . . The students used to have rice once a week, but we have since canceled this as it is not readily available on the market. We have discovered that there is need for us to be thankful that we can provide a plate of sadza for each of them daily. We are living what it really means to thank God for the "daily bread" since we cannot tell where our next batch of corn meal will come from after what we have stored is finished.

Most of us do not worry about food provisions for tomorrow. The local grocery store remains fully stocked, always open, and fairly affordable. Fast-food chains and restaurants dot the landscape in abundance so we can get something to eat or drink at a moment's notice. Indeed, we have such an availability of food that obesity has become a major national health concern.

It hardly seems that we need to pray, "Give us this day our daily bread." Yet N. T. Wright warns that "the danger with the prayer for bread is that we get there too soon."[2] We want to jump straight to our needs—often health or financial issues—rather than begin with God's will and kingdom, without recognizing the importance of our community, our adoption into the Father's family, and His life-shaping holiness. Our needs—our *daily* needs—can feel so pressing and so urgent that we hurry to them without adequate perspective of the heavenly realm.

Prayer for our physical and material needs sometimes becomes the *only* way we pray, and it focuses our attention solely on us. When they share in prayer, many groups of believers create shopping lists of surgeries, aches, pains, financial hardships, and special needs they face. When did you last hear people spontaneously pray that God's name be honored throughout all creation, that they yearn for the coming of His kingdom, and willingly lay down their own hopes, dreams, desires, and ambitions that His will might be accomplished through them? Such prayer is rare, though Jesus gave us such a pattern to live by.

Nevertheless, the Prayer now turns to our daily bread, and we can be very grateful.

The Lord's Prayer has already included three petitions (Hallowed be your name; your kingdom come; your will be done) and now begins the second triad of petitions (for bread, forgiveness, and deliverance). In some ways, this request for bread seems far too mundane for such a powerful and profound prayer. Indeed, *daily* bread—which immediately makes us aware that the Prayer is a *daily* prayer—seems altogether too ordinary. Yet Dale Allison asserts that this fourth petition of the Lord's Prayer is "the most difficult and controversial of the petitions."[3] Really? Apparently.

> *Daily bread seems altogether too ordinary.*

Throughout Christian history, believers and scholars have worked this petition in all directions, spiritualizing the daily bread (more often than not) to mean the Lord's Supper, the Messianic banquet of the end times, the spiritual bread of Christ himself, or a handful of other possibilities.[4] Could Jesus have possibly meant "feed us today with real food for our bodies"?

This fourth petition provides an earthly anchor to this heavenly Prayer. It captures our attention and refuses to let us drift into a purely mystical realm. If we feel tempted to speak of God's holiness, kingdom, and will in otherworldly terms, this petition brings us back to earth. As George Morrison has noted, "On the one side [of this statement in the Prayer] is the will of God, reaching out into the height of heaven. On the other side . . . are our sins, reaching down into unfathomed depths. And then, between these two infinities, spanning the distance from cherubim to Satan, is 'Give us this day our daily bread.'"[5]

This short, earthy request corrects any effort on our part to separate the sacred and the secular. Daily bread bridges any gap we may create or encourage between the spiritual and the material. Thus this fourth petition—the hinge of the prayer in many ways—guides us to consider the materiality of our lives.

The Physical and the Spiritual

Paul Hiebert called it the "excluded middle."[6] He meant that in Western culture we tend to separate the spiritual from the physical. We believe in both, but don't usually see the connections between the two. Thus we view sickness in terms of viruses and bacteria not demons or spiritual principalities. We attribute our financial success (if we have any) to hard work, good education, or good contacts but not the Lord's orchestration. This way of thinking has many telltale signs. We rush to doctors not prayer. We spend enormous amounts of our time trying to make more money, always needing just a little more. We look after the physical. God looks after the spiritual. In practice, that means we look after the here and trust Him mainly with the hereafter. Or we handle the tangible and appeal to Him for the intangible (peace, joy, patience).

This separation of the physical from the spiritual undermines our Christian walk in a range of ways.

Many believers today grow skeptical if we suggest that a broken marriage, a bankruptcy, or a sickness may be the result of spiritual warfare. Despite the fact that Jesus regularly confronted demons that exhibited physical manifestations in people—convulsions, dumbness, violence—we struggle to believe that the spiritual and the physical have intimate connections. Yes, the apostle Paul noted that "our struggle is not against flesh and blood, but against the rulers, against the authorities, against the powers of this dark world and against the spiritual forces of evil in the heavenly realms" (Ephesians 6:12), but he would never deny that the spiritual powers interact with our flesh and blood. They do. Our blindness to the inseparable relationship between the spiritual and the material prevents us from discerning the root of an issue and acting wisely.

We demonstrate our isolation of the physical from the spiritual in other ways, too. Relatively few believers view their everyday employment as a spiritual act of service to the Lord. We seldom see our financial giving as a spiritual exercise, and we tend to define worship in terms of prayer, Bible study, singing, or church attendance. Do simple acts of kindness or compassion—done because we love Christ—qualify as worship? If the love of Christ compels us, can helping a neighbor with their yard work or sitting with someone in a hospital be an expression of worship? Absolutely. Particularly when we serve others as a way to serve Christ. We ascribe worth to Him, the most basic definition of worship.

We regularly claim that spiritual leadership in the home means leading in devotional activities, such as prayer and discussion of Scripture. But might spiritual leadership equally involve creating an environment of acceptance, safety, and joy by eating together, laughing together, providing, protecting, respecting, loving each other, as well as affirming our faith? Many husbands and fathers feel discouraged and defeated by the expectation that spiritual leadership means the implementation of spiritual disciplines and the assumption that anything less than these disciplines fails the *spiritual* test.

But surely spiritual leadership also involves reflecting the character of the Father so that our families see Him through us. Thus everything we do in the physical realm has spiritual connections.

> *Everything about His life combined the physical and the spiritual seamlessly.*

Jesus taught the principles of the kingdom but He also fed the crowds. He urged a higher moral code, and He healed the sick. He prayed to the Father, and He ate leisurely with tax collectors and prostitutes. Everything about His life combined the physical and the spiritual seamlessly. Would we say that His life constantly vacillated between the spiritual and the material?

Or might we begin to see that we cannot—indeed, must not—disconnect the two?

Give us this day our daily bread.

Our tendency to isolate the spiritual from the material is not new. Indeed, it gave rise to some of the earliest heresies in the church. Before the end of the first century, a movement took shape claiming that Jesus could not possibly have come in the flesh but only *seemed* to do so.[7] After all, a spiritual and perfect God could not truly become a physical and mortal being. The church of the second century fought battles against another version of this teaching—that everything in the material world is *evil* and only the spiritual world is *good*.[8] This false teaching, argued against by John in his first epistle,[9] attracted a large following—and still does.

The chief and most obvious danger of such thinking is compartmentalization of our lives. We have physical, mental, emotional, and spiritual elements of our lives and nurture each one differently. For our physical well-being, we eat, exercise, and sleep (perhaps too much of the first and too little of the latter). For our mental lives, we pursue education (or crosswords and Sudoku). We sometimes place our emotional health in the hands of professional counselors, and go to pastors for spiritual guidance. We find different professionals to help with our different needs. We also have roles and places in our lives that rarely intersect—work, church, and home.

This process harms us. We fail to live with integrity—in the sense of wholeness (an *integer* is a whole number)—and we pay a high price for it because a fragmented, disconnected life falls short of the consistent and all-encompassing abundant life that Christ intends for us. As one part of us suffers, all parts suffer. And here, in the middle of the Prayer, Jesus inserts a strategic request: *Give us this day our daily bread.*

The connections between the spiritual and the material run deep. For example, the apostle Paul understood that even our sexuality has deep spiritual undercurrents.

> Do you not know that your bodies are members of Christ himself? Shall I then take the members of Christ and unite them with a prostitute? Never! Do you not know that he who unites himself with a prostitute is one with her in body? For it is said, "The two will become one flesh." . . . Flee from sexual immorality. . . . Do you not know that your body is a temple of the Holy Spirit, who is in you, whom you have received from God? You are not your own; you were bought at a price. Therefore honor God with your body.
>
> 1 Corinthians 6:15–20

Contrary to the popular teaching of our day, sexual encounters are not momentary. They always have spiritual consequences that touch us more deeply than we realize. Sexual immorality does not consecrate the temple of the Holy Spirit but desecrates it—not because the Father is embarrassed by our actions but because our actions bind us spiritually to our partner. Our physical intimacy also involves spiritual intimacy, which can only be healthy in the context of covenant and commitment.

Thus this request for daily bread immediately speaks to us of the connections between the material and the spiritual. Just when we might become preoccupied with the abstract and ethereal in our recitation of the Prayer—appealing for God's will and kingdom—this petition helps us connect the earthly and the heavenly in ways that we might otherwise resist. But the request for daily bread also challenges our inclination to independence.

Learning Dependence

Most of us don't need daily bread; at least not in the same desperate sense that the Israelites, newly arrived in the wilderness out of Egypt, urgently needed sustenance (see Exodus 16). We've got plenty of bread . . . and milk, cereal, meat, vegetables, fruit, cookies, and ice cream. And what we haven't got, we can run to the shops and buy. As William Willimon writes, "Most of us perish from too much bread rather than too little, filling the gnawing emptiness within through ceaseless consumption."[10]

> None *of the Lord's Prayer makes sense when we live self-sufficient and comfortable lives.*

If we're short of cash, we've got credit. We need long-term security, not daily bread. But just when this part of the Prayer seems exclusively applicable to those in deep poverty (people without a refrigerator, a pantry, or a bank account), a shaft of light breaks through the fog of our thinking.

None of the Lord's Prayer makes sense when we live self-sufficient and comfortable lives. And this brief petition (midway through the prayer) jolts us awake. It exposes our independence and raises a question: Does our lack of *daily need* contribute to a *daily neglect* of the Father? The word *daily* gives this petition a distinct frequency and urgency.[11]

As too many of us can attest, occasional attentiveness to the Father produces spiritual lethargy, and those who feel they have the least need often prove to be least attentive. If today's provisions are already in hand, we can get back to the Lord later. But that's precisely what elevates the significance of these seven words.

Give us this day our daily bread.

Just as we're about to ignore it, the utterance challenges whether we *ever* need the Father. Is He a pleasant acquaintance or the very breath of our daily existence?

Furthermore, Jesus confronts our constant efforts to build barns and store up for the future. Daily bread provided by the Father—much as He sent manna for forty years while Israel wandered in the Negev—ought to be enough. But for most of us it's not.

Our retirement planning grows increasingly important. Investments, savings, nest eggs, life insurance, equity, capital, stocks, bonds, and mutual funds can distract us from lives of daily devotion and dependence. We want to leave a financial legacy for our children to "set them up" for better lives than we ourselves had, thinking that it's our effort that matters and that it's our resources they most need.

"Give us *this day* our daily bread."

How do the affluent who take comfort and confidence in their abundance pray such a prayer? Jesus' inclusion of this modest appeal aligns with His earlier statements in the Sermon on the Mount: "Blessed are the poor in spirit . . . those who mourn . . . those who hunger . . . those who are persecuted" (Matthew 5:3–10).

Just as we're about to skip past this unnecessary request for daily bread, we realize that this simple statement presents an indictment of our independence.

Needs and Desires

We might also observe that Jesus taught His disciples to pray for their most basic need, not their most fanciful desire. Bread formed the staple diet in ancient Israel, as it still does for so many people alive today. From the Jewish *challah* to the Moroccan *rghifa*, the French *baguettes* to the Italian *focaccia*, every culture has a basic bread. But "Give us this day our daily bread" draws attention to our needs more than our wants.

> *I have no business asking for surplus in a world marked by poverty.*

Mahatma Gandhi once said, "Earth provides enough to satisfy every man's need, but not every man's greed."[12] I'd like to pray for loads of exotic foods and extravagant desserts, but the Prayer reminds me that I have no business asking for surplus in a world marked by poverty. We may pray earnestly for a house, a car, money to cover our credit card bills, a musical instrument, and a thousand other desires of our heart. But Jesus teaches us to pray for bread.

We'd also like to pray for a year's supply at a time. That would certainly ease the worry and tension we might feel. Who wants to be a day laborer, earning just enough today to eat today? What if something goes wrong? We judge it best to always have a buffer, some savings to fall back on. And that makes good sense. But it's not what Jesus invited us to pray for. Indeed, almost immediately after presenting the Prayer, Jesus goes on to say:

> No one can serve two masters. Either he will hate the one and love the other, or he will be devoted to the one and despise the other. You cannot serve both God and Money. Therefore I tell you, do not worry about your life, what you will eat or drink; or about your body, what you will wear. Is not life more important than food, and the body more important than clothes? Look at the birds of the air; they do not sow or reap or store away in barns, and yet your heavenly Father feeds them. Are you not much more valuable than they? Who of you by worrying can add a single hour to his life? . . . But seek first his kingdom and his righteousness, and all these things will be given to you as well. Therefore do not worry about tomorrow, for tomorrow will worry about itself. Each day has enough trouble of its own.

Matthew 6:24–34

143

Most of what we request in prayer is superfluous to our daily *need*. We adopt a certain lifestyle and standard of living, we choose a certain place to live, we commit ourselves to certain expenses and purchases, but if we appraise it honestly we would have to say that many of these adoptions, choices, and commitments fall outside the realm of *need*. Do we need cell phones, high-speed Internet connections, high-definition televisions, cable programming, walk-in closets full of clothing, restaurant dining, new cars, and more?

On another occasion, Mahatma Gandhi put simplicity into perspective: "Live simply, that others might simply live."[13] In a sense, that's the sentiment undergirding this prayerful petition: "Lord, simplify our demands and expectations. Help us with what we need, today, so that we might help others whose needs will not be met today." This short petition not only redirects our attention away from our own extravagance—and perhaps waste—but it also opens our hearts to those whose needs we might meet.

The Compassionate Heart

"Give *us* this day our daily bread." For only the second time in the Prayer we encounter a first-person-plural pronoun—*us*. The first was at the opening: "*Our* Father." It speaks loudly not only to our personal need but to our collective need. This is the petition that promotes compassion.

St. Basil the Great, the fourth-century Bishop of Caesarea, concluded that nothing we have is ours alone:

The bread that is spoiling in your house belongs to the hungry. The shoes that are mildewing under your bed belong to those who have none. The clothes stored away in your trunk belong to those who are naked. The money that depreciates in your treasury belongs to the poor![14]

When Jesus teaches *us* to pray for *our* daily bread, it becomes a prayer with a lateral glance. My request cannot be for me alone, but for all of us who may pray this together. Indeed, the net may be cast even wider and include all of humanity. As we seek God's will to be done on earth as it is in heaven, how can we conclude that this petition for daily bread concerns itself only with our individual needs?

Give us this day our daily bread. For those in Zimbabwe in 2007, these words became a very serious and literal plea. Christian pastors in training gratefully received a plate of sadza each day. For those of us in the West, the words are no less serious as they invite us to connect the physical and spiritual worlds more closely, to learn deeper dependence upon Christ each day, to clarify our needs and our wants, and to live compassionately toward each other.

CHAPTER 8

Forgive Us Our Debts As We Also Have Forgiven Our Debtors

Nurturing a Culture of Grace

Forgive us our debts as we also have forgiven our debtors.

Simon Wiesenthal, in his classic book *The Sunflower,*[1] introduces us to an ethical dilemma. During the days of the Holocaust, Wiesenthal—a Jew—found himself at the bedside of a dying German soldier who pleaded for forgiveness for all the heinous acts he had committed against the Jews. The soldier lay in his bed conscience-stricken and unprepared for eternity. Wiesenthal listened to the testimony of the man and received the request, but quietly turned and left the room without offering absolution. In *The Sunflower,* Wiesenthal defends his decision not to forgive the man, and the book includes a dialogue with various philosophers and others about whether they agree with his actions or not—and why.

Irrespective of what we may have done if thrust into that wrenching circumstance, the book touches the heart because it speaks to a need we all feel on a regular basis: the need for forgiveness.

Ravi Zacharias tells the story of a time he visited India and saw a crowd hurrying to a small roadside shrine. A Brahman priest stood there, decked in his finery. Someone stepped forward with a small goat, and with a deft action, the priest slipped a knife from its scabbard and slit the throat of the animal. The priest then dabbed the fresh blood on the forehead of the man who had brought the goat. Zacharias felt stunned by the violence. He watched the crowd dissipate as quickly as it had formed, then he approached the priest. "Why did you do that?" The priest had no interest in a conversation with this stranger. He muttered, "Get away! Get away!" On later reflection, Zacharias found himself moved by the most fundamental need of the human heart—for absolution.

No wonder, then, that Jesus includes a plea to the Father for forgiveness in this powerful Prayer. Yet we seldom seem stricken by the state of our hearts. When the wheels get completely loose or fall off our life's wagon, we may admit fault or responsibility and plead for a fresh start. But relatively few believers live with a profound sense of their indebtedness to God.

We Languish

> Listen to the word of the LORD . . . for the LORD has a case
> against the inhabitants of the land, because there is no
> faithfulness or kindness or knowledge of God in the land.
> There is swearing, deception, murder, stealing and adultery.
> They employ violence, so that bloodshed follows bloodshed.
> Therefore the land mourns, and everyone who lives in it
> languishes.
>
> Hosea 4:1–3 NASB

Languish. Synonyms abound for this rich English word:
droop, fade, grow indifferent, listless, weak, and feeble. It's
exactly what the ancient prophet Hosea wanted to say. The
people of Israel had grown complacent about life, each other,
and sin. Nothing really mattered—not their word, not their
neighbors, not marriages, not civility.

As Hosea sought to describe the pitiful state of his day, he
chose a Hebrew word that translates well as "languish." And
the message he delivered 2,750 years ago
still strikes with considerable force.

The very offenses Hosea identified in Israel have become the stuff of our entertainment.

The very offenses Hosea identified in
Israel have become the stuff of our entertainment. Swearing, deception, murder,
stealing, adultery, and violence form the
subplots to our movies and the grist for
our daily news. And we languish.

It's not that we approve such things. Rather they intrigue
us and draw us like moths to a flame. The sin of our culture

has ceased to horrify us and now titillates us. Gradually, perhaps imperceptibly, we grow blind to "righteousness and justice . . . love and compassion" (Hosea 2:19), and the vices we tolerate inoculate us from abundant life. We languish, which is precisely the reason that Jesus in His wisdom builds confession and forgiveness into the Prayer.

Sin undermines our intimacy with Christ. Always has, always will. Our denial of it, indifference to it, or tolerance of it limits the depths to which we can know Him and the Father. When cursing and lies become the norm, when life is cheap and marriage is meaningless, when violence thrills us rather than grieves us, our hearts stiffen and our spirits wilt. We languish.

Tragically, Israel never heeded Hosea's warning. They stumbled about in a spiritual daze, blinded by the toxic effect of their collective and private sin. They refused to recognize or repent of it and the outcome was devastating—a ruined land and a listless people.

Sin still seduces us, until what we call "life" deteriorates into a pale reflection of what the Father intended. In our pursuit of godliness, ruthless surgery on our sin becomes foundational. The Lord said to Israel: "I will go back to my place until they admit their guilt. And they will seek my face; in their misery they will earnestly seek me" (Hosea 5:15).

We dare not neglect an appeal to the Father for forgiveness. However, such an appeal must be predicated on a genuine awareness of the debt we owe.

Preconditions for Forgiveness?

Forgive us our debts as we also have forgiven our debtors.

The Prayer challenges us with each phrase, but on the topic of forgiveness it seems to contradict a very basic biblical teaching: the unconditional love of God.

As we appeal to God for forgiveness, Jesus adds a disturbing clause. He forgives us *when* or *because* or *in the same way that we have already forgiven others.* His forgiveness has a condition attached. Worse still—it's a *pre*condition.

Paul Tournier writes: "So far as a human being is concerned, caught up in the drama of guilt, a God who does not forgive can no longer be regarded as a God who loves unconditionally; and a God who lays down conditions for His forgiveness does the same for His love."[2]

> How dare we beg for grace with no intention of extending that same grace to others.

I can forgive some folk and some offenses relatively easily. But serious injuries and grievances take a while. And just when I think I've moved on, something triggers a response from me that shows I have not forgiven as fully as I thought. My capacity to forgive others seems inconsistent and incomplete at best. Will God's forgiveness be the same for me? The thought is horrifying!

Forgive us our debts *as we also have forgiven our debtors.* Is this really a precondition? Or does Christ use this opportunity to reaffirm that kingdom life flourishes when we both offer and receive forgiveness?

The hyperbole—exaggeration to make a point—achieves its goal. It shocks us. How dare we beg for grace with no intention of extending that same grace to others. How impudent of us to plead for forgiveness while harboring bitterness and resentment against others.

Christ knows that guilt eats us from two directions. Our own guilt before God burdens us, but so does the relentless condemnation we cast on others—in our marriages, families, workplaces, churches, and neighborhoods. Both scenarios destroy us.

Jesus also told a searing parable of an ungrateful servant. This ingrate stands as an eternal warning to each of us.

> The kingdom of God is like a king who decided to square accounts with his servants. As he got under way, one servant was brought before him who had run up a debt of a hundred thousand dollars. He couldn't pay up, so the king ordered the man, along with his wife, children, and goods, to be auctioned off at the slave market. The poor wretch threw himself at the king's feet and begged, "Give me a chance and I'll pay it all back." Touched by his plea, the king let him off, erasing the debt.
>
> The servant was no sooner out of the room when he came upon one of his fellow servants who owed him ten dollars. He seized him by the throat and demanded, "Pay up. Now!" The poor wretch threw himself down and begged, "Give me a chance and I'll pay it all back." But he wouldn't do it. He had him arrested and put in jail until the debt was paid. When the other servants saw this going

on, they were outraged and brought a detailed report to the king.

The king summoned the man and said, "You evil servant! I forgave your entire debt when you begged me for mercy. Shouldn't you be compelled to be merciful to your fellow servant who asked for mercy?" The king was furious and put the screws to the man until he paid back his entire debt. And that's exactly what my Father in heaven is going to do to each one of you who doesn't forgive unconditionally anyone who asks for mercy.

Matthew 18:23–35 The Message

The first servant's request, "Give me a chance!" rested on the sands of hypocrisy as he refused to have mercy on others. He wanted personal absolution of his own debt without fostering a culture of grace, and the kingdom has no place for such duplicity.

In the Sermon on the Mount, Jesus urged His listeners: "If you are offering your gift at the altar and there remember that your brother has something against you, leave your gift there in front of the altar. First go and be reconciled to your brother; then come and offer your gift" (Matthew 5:23–24).

Jesus invites us into a culture and circle of forgiveness.

Forgive us our debts as we also have forgiven our debtors. The Lord does *not* demand a precondition to His love. However, by means of the hyperbole (and the Sermon on the Mount is full of hyperbole, e.g., Matthew 5:29–30) Jesus invites us into a culture and circle of forgiveness. This prayerful plea challenges our presumptuous attitudes and guides us to reconciled relationships.

Forgiving and Forgetting

Interestingly, Jesus does not pray, "Forgive *and forget* our debts as we have forgiven *and forgotten* the debts of others." We forgive, but don't necessarily forget.

We usually receive quite different advice, especially in Christian circles. Many people would have us forgive *and forget*. Others might even suggest that we have not truly forgiven until we forget. But how much conflict do we revisit because we have forgotten or been in denial about the past?

> *We forgive, but don't necessarily forget.*

The abused wife, desperate for a good marriage and a loving husband, may deny the severity of the abuse she has endured. But her efforts to block the memories can only lead to further heartache. Denial of the past simply assures repetition in the future.

Yes, the apostle Paul wrote that love "keeps no record of wrongs" (1 Corinthians 13:5). Was he suggesting that true godliness has selective amnesia? If so, it's hard to understand God's preserving a written and detailed record in the Bible of so many human failings of the past—by individuals and nations—many of which He forgave.

The dangers of forgetting are significant.

Without a clear memory, we have little ability to break the destructive cycles in marriages, families, and churches.

Accountability depends on memory. Forgetting does little to challenge the perpetrator or change the future.

Surely the point of Paul's comment that love keeps no record of wrongs is that we keep no record for punitive purposes. Love does not dredge up the past so that it can repeatedly punish someone. But our memory is strategic to our growth, even our spiritual growth.

When God removes our sins as far as the east is from the west, He affirms that He will not continually hold them against us. His declaration to "remember their sins no more" (Jeremiah 31:34) does not suggest forgetfulness—can the all-knowing Creator forget anything?—but a choice not to sustain the offense. In contrast, we read in Jeremiah 14:10: "This is what the LORD says about this people: 'They greatly love to wander; they do not restrain their feet. So the LORD does not accept them; *he will now remember their wickedness and punish them for their sins.*" The Lord now remembers for a specific purpose, to administer judgment. Jeremiah affirms that the Lord's "memory" has to do with visiting punishment.

Our forgetfulness at the political and international level has definitely hindered any consistent response to genocide and brutality in the world. In our churches, divisive cycles repeat themselves endlessly, usually every five to seven years, when we fail to address them intentionally. Furthermore, forgetfulness undermines our capacity to anticipate future problems, resolve conflicts, or guide people to a healthier future. In our marriages, forgetfulness or denial almost guarantees repetition of conflict.

Remembering an offense does not render us unchristian or ungodly, though we have no right to repeatedly raise an issue to wound someone. In fact, we might find that overlooking, denying, or forgetting a destructive or harmful moment can prove hazardous.

We choose not to exact revenge when we could; that's forgiveness. But we dare not forget, lest we—or, more important, others—be victimized again. And in our memory, guided by grace and lathered with the love of the Father, lies our strongest future.

Indeed, this portion of the Prayer—perhaps more than any other—steers us toward experiencing the Father's grace. As we appeal for His forgiveness, we know full well that we can do nothing to "make it right" with Him. We fall so far short of His plan and desire for us. Thus we appeal to grace.

Some people define this grace as *undeserved favor.* I suspect that we do better justice to Scripture when we define it as *receiving the opposite of what we deserve.* We deserve punishment; we receive blessing. We deserve judgment;

> *Grace is receiving the opposite of what we deserve.*

we receive adoption. We deserve alienation; we receive welcome. The challenge for any of us who receive such grace is to live in it fully and then extend it to others.

Over the years I have found that one way to determine whether a person lives in grace or law is to listen to their language.

Watching Our Language

We want to watch our language in several ways. Cuss words, off-color jokes, and crudity—as we noted in the chapter on holiness—may reflect hearts needing surgery. But a more subtle and sinister language slips straight through our defenses and can prove just as harmful.

The language that courses through the Christian bloodstream and threatens to undermine the gospel in our lives is the language of law, and many believers demonstrate alarming fluency in this destructive dialect.

The language of law repeatedly uses terms of obligation, duty, and demand. Listen to yourself speak. Read what you write and look for terms like *should, ought, have to, need to,* and *must.* I *should* do more Bible study. I *ought* to pray more. I *must* do more in ministry. I *need to* be more compassionate. Every statement reflects the language of obligation and does little more than compound our guilt and lessen our joy.

Some years ago a ministry student of mine called and asked if he might visit. When he arrived we chatted casually for a few minutes before I asked, "So tell me, how's your ministry?" Peter's body language changed dramatically. He could barely make eye contact with me. His shoulders slumped as he studied the carpet, and the words began to flow: "I'm not doing well. I should be out visiting more. I need to be doing more sermon preparation. Actually, I ought to take another preaching course. The congregation tells me that I have to be more of a leader." And so the torrent continued. Every sentence contained a law phrase: *should, need to, ought to, have to,* and the like. I stopped Peter during his catharsis. "Peter, let's start this conversation all over again. But this time, reframe your ministry in terms of what you'd *like* to do, *hope* to do, *want* to do, *desire* to do." He fell silent. Words simply would not come. I briefly pointed out his victimization to the law, and he left without much more conversation. It was nearly twelve months later before he returned for a follow-up visit, smiling and filled with joy. His first words: "I've discovered the freedom of living in grace!"

Why do so many of us speak about grace but actually live by the law? We tout freedom in Christ but live oppressed by the duties (and failures) of the faith. Real grace and liberation will result in (and may be the result of) a new language.

The language of grace uses a different set of terms. I *want* to read more. I'd *like* to give. I *desire* to serve. I *choose* to pray. Only as we voice this latter language will the shackles of the law begin to loosen and the freedom of the gospel begin to flood our hearts like a burst dam pouring into the valley below. It sounds so simple, replacing one range of words with another and resisting the bondage of duty.

I'm not suggesting that followers of Christ have no obligation or duty. Of course we do. Christ gave us commands, not suggestions, for following Him. Yet when we approach them from the perspective of a burden (what we *have* to do) rather than a joy (what we *want* to do) we inevitably feel resistance and resentment.

As we watch our language, especially the insidious law language that seems endemic to the gospel community, we'll not only enjoy forgiveness and freedom ourselves but we'll begin extending it to others. The world criticizes the church with good cause when we proclaim good news and then beat ourselves constantly with terms of obligation, duty, and demand.

A huge step forward for all of us might come as we employ grace language, and we learn this language as we nurture the culture of grace. "Forgive us our debts as we also have forgiven our debtors." As we genuinely forgive others we'll speak differently of them and allow them to live in grace, even as we desire to live in grace.

Forgiveness Frees Us

We cannot overstate the liberation of forgiveness. Resentment and bitterness twist us out of shape, but forgiveness restores us and allows us to move on.

> *Forgiveness restores us and allows us to move on.*

A friend of mine patrols a suburban Los Angeles neighborhood. He's a Christian policeman who takes seriously Christ's call for him to be salt and light in the midst of a very dark world—and the police see a darkness that most of us do not. Recently he was assigned to visit a home and remove two children from their mother. The mother's failure to provide adequate care put the well-being of the children at risk, and the children—an eight-month-old baby and a seven-year-old girl—needed to be taken to a foster-care organization. The young girl, mature beyond her years, sat quietly in the police cruiser. My friend struck up a conversation with her. "What do you like best about school?" he asked. The young girl replied, "Learning about God." He had really not expected that response. The young girl was apparently mixing up her regular school and her Sunday school experiences, but he just carried the conversation along. "So, what's your favorite Bible story?" His seven-year-old passenger responded, "The one about the wise king and the two mothers who came to him. One was the real mother and the other was not. The king [Solomon—see 1 Kings 3] decided to cut the baby in half and give half to each woman, but the real mother couldn't stand to see her child die, so she offered to give up the child rather than see it die." My friend, perhaps like us, could hardly imagine why such a story would be a favorite of this elementary-school kid. "Why do you like that story so much?" "Because it reminds me of my own mom—that sometimes the most loving thing she can do is give us up for our own good."

Our hearts may grieve that a seven-year-old should have such a sophisticated understanding of a Bible story. But she harbored no bitterness toward her mother. Indeed, she found forgiveness in her heart for her mother, and that forgiveness allowed her to live with a measure of freedom.

The power of forgiveness lies not only in our being forgiven—the joy of absolution—but also in our forgiving others. When we harbor grudges and resentment against others, they become leg-irons that restrict our movements and cut into our flesh.

The anonymous writer to the Hebrews put it this way: "See to it that no one misses the grace of God and that no bitter root grows up to cause trouble and defile many" (Hebrews 12:15). When we miss grace, we feed bitterness. And the outcome of bitterness, pictured as a root that buries deep into our hearts and establishes itself, is trouble and defilement. If we want to grow in the knowledge and the grace of Christ and experience freedom to live life to the full as the Father intends, we'll want to cut off that root and learn the grace of forgiveness.

> *When we miss grace, we feed bitterness.*

Presuming Forgiveness

Emo Philips once quipped: "When I was a kid I used to pray every night for a new bicycle. Then I realized that the Lord doesn't work that way, so I stole one and asked Him to forgive me."[3] We might smile at his rationalization, but many of us believe that it's easier to ask for forgiveness than permission. We presume upon the goodwill of God and others.

The apostle Paul knew our propensity to abuse grace. If we know that we'll be forgiven, we're more likely to offend. It's human nature—fallen nature. We presume upon forgiveness. Consequently, Paul addressed this tendency head on. "What shall we say, then? Shall we go on sinning so that grace may increase? By no means! We died to sin; how can we live in it any longer?" (Romans 6:1–2).

Certain people in the early church distorted the teaching of grace, turning it into a license to live as they liked. They distorted God's pure gift and apparently taught that the more we sin the more grace He extends—which means the more glory He gets. What a strange justification of sin. The worse we are the better He looks, so let's do our best to make Him look *really* good!

I've not met anyone in recent times who genuinely believes such nonsense. But I've met many people who practice a milder version of it. "We can always come back to Him. No matter what we do or how we live, He will always forgive us." And such thinking can produce a lax discipleship. It results in what Dallas Willard describes as "sin management."[4] That is, we manage our sin just enough to live our own way without riling up God too much, like children who know just how far to push their parents before they cross the line. Sin management, therefore, minimizes our punishment while allowing us to indulge the fallen nature. We take some care not to cross the line, which could have disastrous consequences, but feel relatively comfortable approaching the line. God's faithfulness and consistency become a spiritual return policy that allows us to offer a brief apology and have full restoration of all privileges, promises, and benefits that we feel entitled to in the kingdom. But we walk on thin ice when we presume upon His forgiveness.

Forgive us our debts as we have forgiven our debtors. As we pray this Prayer and enter into the culture of grace we realize that we not only receive forgiveness but also give it. How do we feel about other people who push us right to the limit and then after a quick apology expect everything to be okay? None of us like to be treated that way. Such presumptuous behavior does nothing to deepen our mutual respect or relationship. Nor does it help our walk with the Father.

Confession of sin cannot be casual. Repentance cannot be flippant. A. W. Tozer described the veil that stands between us and God as made up of "the fine threads of the self-life, the hyphenated sins of the human spirit . . . self-righteousness, self-pity, self-confidence, self-sufficiency, self-admiration, self-love, and a host of others like them."[5] This veil must be torn asunder. Yet

> *Confession of sin cannot be casual. Repentance cannot be flippant.*

> . . . to tear it away is to injure us, to hurt us and make us bleed. To say otherwise is to make the cross no cross and death no death at all. It is never fun to die. . . . The cross is rough and it is deadly, but it is effective. It does not keep its victim hanging there forever. There comes a moment when its work is finished and the suffering victim dies. After that is resurrection glory and power, and the pain is forgotten for joy that the veil is taken away and we have entered in actual spiritual experience the presence of the living God.[6]

Forgive us. The phrase, uttered from contrite and sincere lips, acknowledges our sin, invites its crucifixion, and awaits resurrection. It also affirms our commitment to foster a culture of grace—offering freely to others what we ourselves desire and receive from the Father.

CHAPTER 9

= Lead Us Not Into Testing, = but Deliver Us From the Evil

Growing in Faith and Obedience

Lead us not into testing, but deliver us from the evil.

We memorized this portion of the Prayer differently— "Lead us not into *temptation,* but deliver us from evil"—but we have good reason to modify the translation.

This petition forms the final request of the Lord's Prayer. Hereafter, the Prayer closes with a magnificent, triumphant affirmation of the sovereignty of God. But in this moment, Jesus turns our attention to the grim reality of evil. No prayer is genuinely complete that ignores the struggles of our fallen world, the titanic battle between good and evil that rages around us and within us. Since the garden of Eden, evil has lurked in the shadows of our hearts and sin has conspired to destroy us. The warning that the Lord gave to Cain remains urgent for us: "Sin is crouching at your door; it desires to have you, but you must master it" (Genesis 4:7). As much as ever, we need to pray, "Deliver us from the evil." But before deliverance from the evil, Jesus teaches us to pray, "Lead us not into temptation / testing."

Temptations and Tests

When Jesus thought of testing and "the evil," He probably recalled His own personal encounter with Satan forty days after His baptism. That incident occurred just a short while before Jesus taught this Prayer. The three great tests that the devil presented after that wilderness retreat surely left an indelible impression on Jesus. How could anyone forget such an experience? However, our English translations of that story raise a tough question for us when we come to this part of the Lord's Prayer, since most of our translations indicate that the Spirit of God led Jesus into the wilderness "to be *tempted* by the devil" (Matthew 4:1).[1] Does God tempt us?

Does God tempt us?

The problem is highlighted as we compare three New Testament passages. In each instance, the author uses the same Greek word—*peirasmos*.[2] The Spirit led Jesus into the desert to be *tempted* (see Matthew 4:1). The Lord *tested* Abraham when He asked Abraham to sacrifice his son Isaac (see Hebrews 11:17). And James writes, "When *tempted* no one should say,

'God is *tempting* me.' For God cannot be *tempted* by evil, *nor does He tempt anyone*" (James 1:13).

Does God tempt us or not?

Is there a difference between temptation and a test? To most of our minds, yes. *Temptation* usually carries connotations of something that crosses a moral line—tempted to steal, lust, envy, or lie, for example. When we say that we feel sorely tempted, we generally mean that we feel strongly inclined to violate the moral code of the kingdom, though we also might feel sorely tempted by a slice of pecan pie!

A test, however, relates more to our faith. Much like Abraham, we may feel that various trials and hardships test whether or not we will trust the Father.

It's this latter aspect of *peirasmos* that often appears throughout the New Testament and best applies to the Prayer. Just as Satan tested Jesus' own trust in the Father, so the Father may test our faith and trust in Him. God does not seduce us to sin (temptation) though He may refine our faith or discipline our disobedience in ways that feel quite difficult at the time.

We can reconcile the apparent conflict with James 1:13 by adding verse 14: "When tempted, no one should say, 'God is tempting me.' For God cannot be tempted by evil, nor does he tempt anyone; *but each one is tempted when, by his own evil desire, he is dragged away and enticed.*" The Father will not appeal to our evil desire nor entice someone into moral failure.

Do not lead us into testing.

We might recall the Israelites, who endured a forty-year period of testing and refining in the wilderness of Sinai after their exodus from Egypt. Or Job. While God did not cause the terrible afflictions that beset Job, He allowed them as a test of his faith.

This theme of testing courses its way throughout the New Testament. Paul wrote to his friends at Corinth: "No temptation [*test;* same word] has seized you except what is common to man. And God is faithful; he will not let you be tempted [*tested;* same word] beyond what you can bear. But when you are tempted [*tested;* same word], he will also provide a way out so that you can stand up under it" (1 Corinthians 10:13). Later Paul would write to those same believers and exhort them, "Examine [*test;* same word] yourselves to see whether you are in the faith" (2 Corinthians 13:5). If God administers the tests, which He often does, it's not so that He might destroy us but refine us.

We don't generally like testing. We probably hated it at school and fear it at the doctor's office. It's hardly something we want in the spiritual realm, though the Father may at times, just like our teachers and our doctors, administer tests for our own good. Nevertheless, Jesus urges us to pray, "Lead us not into testing." Can we become an answer to our own prayer? Of course we can.

These two words—trust and obedience—form the heart of the biblical idea of faith.

At the doctor's, we avoid testing by showing good health. In our spiritual journey, we can sidestep some of the testing by living lives of deep trust and obedience. These two words—trust and obedience—form the heart of the biblical idea of faith. When we begin to trust ourselves, we may need a test; not that God may pass or fail us, but that we might see our need to restore our trust *in Him*. When we choose the path of disobedience, we may need a test so that we might better gauge the depth or shallowness of our faith and make corrections.[3]

The teaching of the Prayer—and the wider New Testament—encourages us to test ourselves from time to time, to take a faith challenge of our own making, and to always be alert to the possibility of a faith test of the Father's choosing. Such tests are never designed to humiliate or crush us but to restore and regenerate us.

Lead us not into testing simply means *lead us into deeper faith.* As we trust the Father more, the tests become fewer.

As an eight-year-old, Caleb, my middle son, trusted me implicitly. Most parents enjoy a short, blissful period like this. In his mind, I had the strength, power, wisdom, and experience to solve virtually any problem, from opening a can to protecting him on the streets. He saw nothing as a test of his faith in me because he had utter faith in me. But over the years he has grown to doubt my omnipotence—just because he can outwrestle me, outrun me, and outthink me. In the process, I am confident that he does not love me less, but his life experience has seriously tested that youthful, unquestioning trust.

Similarly our life experiences, if we shift our eyes from the Father, can cause us to doubt Him. It's not that we love Him less, but when He doesn't solve all our problems with the urgency or answers we'd like, our trust in Him can waver.

Trust that is based in His performance and not His love always suffers this fate. Thus with time our jaded confidence needs a test. It's not the Lord who needs the test but we. Herein lays the power and necessity of the Prayer. *Lead us not into testing.* As we utter this plea, we don't really appeal for trouble-free lives. Instead we declare to the Father the yearning of our hearts to deepen our trust. "We do believe; help us overcome our unbelief!" (See Mark 9:24.)

Deliver Us From the Evil

The Jews of the first century likely heard this phrase— "Deliver us from the evil"—with clear political undertones. At the Passover Feast each year they remembered the forty years of testing after their four hundred years of slavery in Egypt, though it happened fourteen hundred years earlier. They had felt tested and disciplined many times since as a steady stream of evil occupiers had oppressed them in their own land. "Do not lead us into testing, but deliver us from the evil" took on obvious significance to them in the first century, too. They despised the oppressive Roman occupation of their land. They resented the brutality and violence that produced the *pax Romana.* They feared the threat to their own faith and families. Everyone could identify the "evil." *Father, deliver us from these contemptible Romans.*

In our own day, if we listen to some analysts, we might leap to conclude that radical Islam is "the evil" that most threatens us. The war on terrorism, the threat of al-Qaeda militants, and the bombings and attacks against innocents around the world all feed this fear.

The most insidious and lethal expression of evil, however, lies not in foreign ideologies, tyrannical regimes, or demonic forces in distant places, but within our own hearts. We hesitate to admit it, but we must. Our hearts harbor the very evil we despise most.

Our most mortal enemy is not the one who forces us against our will, but the one who destroys us *by appealing to our will*. It won't help us to muster field-savvy soldiers for this battle. We need spiritual reserves, spiritual reinforcements, and spiritual tactics.

Deliver us from the evil.

Perhaps Jesus refers to "the evil *one*," the devil, which is how the *New International Version* chooses to translate it. If we add *one* to the text, it both clarifies and confines the meaning. However, the original text literally reads, "deliver us from the evil." Might this simply highlight how entrenched, how serious, and how grim is *the* evil within? We all know it.

We don't need theological treatises about original sin or the depravity of humanity. Our everyday reality causes us to cry out like the lepers: "Jesus, Master, have mercy on us!" (Luke 17:13 NASB).

Deliver us from the evil.

If we are serious in our plea, He does—not by destroying every vestige of evil in our culture but by transforming the home of evil in our hearts. Is there a day that we don't need to pray this prayer? Is there a moment when, standing in His light, we don't see more of our own darkness?

Jesus' Prayer surprises us. In our shame and fear we want to ignore the reality of evil within us, lest it provoke the Father's rebuke. But Jesus invites us to name it so the Father can deal with it.

Have you named *the* enemy in your own heart? Evil has many names: anger, lust, jealousy, greed, pride, aggression, bitterness, indifference, to mention just a few, and naming the evil establishes the beachhead for deliverance.

The Enemy Within

In November 2006, amidst great scandal, Ted Haggard, the senior pastor of the 14,000-member New Life Church in Colorado and president of the National Association of Evangelicals, resigned from his ministry. A loud and public critic of homosexuality, he admitted to clandestine motel meetings for massages from a self-confessed gay prostitute.

We might cry, "Hypocrisy!" in this instance, or a thousand just like it, but something deeper beckons our consideration.

Gordon MacDonald wrote in a pastoral note:

When I see a leader who becomes stubborn and rigid . . . less compassionate toward his adversaries [and] increasingly tyrannical . . . I wonder if he is not generating all of this heat because he is trying so hard to say "no" to something surging deep within his own soul. Are his words and deeds not so much directed against an enemy "out there" as they are against a much more cunning enemy within his own soul? More than once I have visited with pastors who have spent hours immersed in pornography and then gone on to preach their most "spirit-filled" sermons against immorality a day or two later.[4]

This phenomenon spans the centuries. William Shakespeare had Queen Gertrude declare, "The lady doth protest too much" in a scene in which a widow kept insisting on her loyalty to her husband.[5]

Excessive protests and overly vigorous opposition sometimes indicate wounds or woundedness within *us*. Indeed, our own pain and failure can generate considerable conviction and passion. Consequently, it may help us to clarify if our fervor and stridency arises because we are sorrowful for people who have fallen or simply struggling with ourselves. A critical spirit may reveal more about our own inner struggles than the shortcomings of others. We should all pause.

Of course, we don't handle the enemy within and around us by resorting to silence. Salt and light must stand out, not blend in. Thus, our pause should not settle into stagnation. Nevertheless, the greatest enemy we face does not live in others but in our own breast. This enemy poses our greatest threat. Yes, we must speak out against oppression, injustice, and immorality. But let's also look within and pray for transformation. Transformation lies at the heart of what Jesus teaches in the Prayer.

Unless change becomes the constant of our own lives, we'll cease to be change agents in the lives of others. And any suggestion that we have no sin will undermine our capacity to touch our families, friends, co-workers, or neighbors.

Before we crusade to tear down the strongholds in others, let's confront our own demons and then speak truth from lives of humility, obedience, and sincerity. Therein lies genuine freedom for us all. And a strategic element of confronting the enemy within is to give it a name.

> *Unless change becomes the constant of our own lives, we'll cease to be change agents in the lives of others.*

Name It

Lead us not into testing, but deliver us from the evil.

Interestingly, Jesus does not identify specific evil. He leaves it unnamed, not because naming lacks importance but because each of us will need to name different evils in our lifetime.

In chapter 4, we noted that a name may describe the character or calling of a person. In biblical times, those who gave the name had authority over what they named. Thus Adam had dominion over the animals and expressed that authority in the act of naming them (see Genesis 2:20). Similarly, parents have authority over their children because they name them. In 2 Kings 23:34, we read that "Pharaoh Neco made Eliakim . . . king in place of his father Josiah *and changed Eliakim's name to Jehoiakim.*" That act of renaming a puppet king sent a signal to everyone that the Egyptian Pharaoh really ruled over Israel. Whenever people spoke the new name of Jehoiakim, they also remembered their overlord, Neco.

In like vein, the naming of evil becomes an important step toward our deliverance from it.

In reality, we tread lightly and reluctantly, afraid to face charges of political incorrectness, insensitivity, judgmentalism, or intolerance. So in the interest of maintaining our social standing and superficial niceties, we avoid calling sin by its name. Yet as any physician will attest, diagnosis is crucial. Until we identify the problem and name it, any effort at treatment will likely be ineffective or even dangerous. An asthmatic attack does not require antibiotics, nor does heart disease require an inhaler. The same applies to our spiritual lives.

The ancient prophets in Israel functioned as spiritual diagnosticians. As the wealthy prospered and the poor suffered, the prophets stepped forward with words like *injustice, immorality,* and *idolatry.* They spoke the names of the diseases and played a vital role in alerting their contemporaries to the spiritual sickness in the land. Their labels need dusting off in our own day.

Ignorance and secrecy continue to conspire together to hold God's people and God's creation in captivity. We cannot treat what we cannot identify, and since the garden of Eden, every human being has suffered spiritual blind spots. We need prophets as much today as ever, though they seldom receive a warm welcome. Perhaps we could become occasional prophets for each other, in love.

If we refuse to tell the doctor that we've had shooting pains down our arm and oppressive weight on our chest, we risk a massive heart attack. Similarly, sin's power lies in secrecy. We fear shining light in the dark corner. What will people think? And in the process, we invite spiritual disease and decline.

The journey to freedom involves not only steps to put on Christ but also steps to put off sin. That means naming it, not to shame each other but to shore each other up. It means confession of the darkness that we harbor in our souls. And we shall be free indeed.

Bill Wilson and Bob Smith, both alcoholics, practiced this principle back in 1935, when they founded Alcoholics Anonymous. They understood that the first step toward recovery required an admission that they were alcoholics. As long as a person denies their problem, they remain enslaved to it. But upon naming it, the journey to recovery can begin. Those early gatherings of AA have turned into a worldwide movement numbering more than two million members.[6]

The Ephesian believers in the first century also modeled this principle. In Acts 19:18–19, we read of their response to the gospel:

> Many of those who believed now came and *openly confessed their evil deeds.* A number who had practiced sorcery brought their scrolls together and burned them publicly. When they calculated the value of the scrolls, the total came to fifty thousand drachmas.[7]

The English translation "openly confessed their evil deeds" probably does not capture the enormity of the moment. Ephesus reveled in its reputation in the ancient world as the center of the magic arts. The Ephesians produced charms, potions, and incantations but believed that if a curse was known it could be broken. Consequently, the magic arts depended upon secrecy for their power. Those who came to Christ now openly declared their magic to break its power. The *New American Standard Bible* captures this better with the translation "those who had believed kept coming, confessing and *disclosing their practices.*"

To know Christ more fully and the Father more intimately requires that we name and confront the enemies within and among us. Such confession becomes the first step toward breaking the stronghold of sin and evil. Furthermore, Jerry Bridges reminds us, "The Christian should never complain of want of ability and power. If we sin, it is because we choose to sin, not because we lack the ability to say no to temptation."[8]

While we identify and openly name evil so as to break its hold in our lives, our motivation ought to be obedience not victory. That statement sounds odd, to say the least, in a Christian culture that speaks so much of victorious Christian living. Yet Jesus did not teach His disciples to pray for victory but for deliverance—*deliver us from the evil*—and the two are quite different.

We may yearn for victory over sin. We can identify habits and patterns in our lives that shame and oppress us. Perhaps it's the quick temper that gets us into trouble with friends all too regularly. Or the envy that sends us on unaffordable shopping sprees. Or the bitterness that poisons our souls. We want to pray, "Lead us not into testing, but deliver us from the evil" and add, "Give me the victory in this area of my life." But it's not about personal victory.

It's Not About Victory

Sin binds us together. We may differ in personality, taste, background, experience, and skill, but sin makes us equals. While some people struggle with anger, others wrestle with lustful demons. Greed seduces some of us, while jealousy and envy afflicts others. Bitterness and unforgiveness rule in some lives, while lies dominate others. And the list continues. Sin respects no one. It aims to destroy us all.

> *We may differ in personality, taste, background, experience, and skill, but sin makes us equals.*

Before long we find that acts and attitudes become habits with vicelike grips. Our many addictions set out to steal, kill, and destroy what God designed for us (see John 10:10). And who among us has not cried out with the apostle Paul, "What a wretched man I am! Who will rescue me from this body of death?" (Romans 7:24). We've all got stuff we want to conquer. But still sin wins.

We listen to sermons and read books about the victorious Christian life. It sounds wonderful and we want it. We'd like to beat back the bad ways and claim success. But as Jerry Bridges notes, one of the main hindrances to dealing with sin is that our attitude toward it is more *self-centered* than *God-centered*.[9]

We show more concern with our own victory over sin than the fact that our sin grieves the heart of God. We want to defeat it with sheer determination and then glory in our achievement. However, we may have misunderstood the essence of sin. Sin is not about breaking the rules but ruining a relationship—our relationship with the Father.

> *Our preoccupation with success hinders our pursuit of holiness.*

Our preoccupation with success hinders our pursuit of holiness. We grow discouraged by our failure to defeat sin chiefly because we are success oriented, not because we know it offends the Father. It might dramatically change our approach if we grasped the biblical truth that God wants us to walk in obedience, not victory. Obedience is oriented toward God; victory is oriented toward ourselves.

The gospel declares that victory over sin belongs to Christ, not us. He has already conquered the power of sin and death (see 1 Corinthians 15:55–57). In another place, the apostle Paul urges us to "count [ourselves] dead to sin but alive to God in Christ Jesus" (Romans 6:11). The cross achieved the victory. Our response is to "not let sin reign in [our] mortal body [nor] obey its evil desires" (Romans 6:12). Instead, we obediently "offer the parts of [our] body to [Christ] as instruments of righteousness" (Romans 6:13b).

As long as we see our sin as "inevitable" and "unbeatable" we will succumb to it. How much better to desire God above everything, quit dwelling on our failure, and make some obedient life choices that will please Him rather than pain Him.

The Prayer teaches us to lean on the Father to lead, guide, and deliver us, not empower us to have a victory of our own. *He* delivers us. We do not conquer sin in our own strength. And such deliverance arises from obedience, not gritty determination for victory.

Deliver us from the evil.

Handling Our Failure

As much as we desire deliverance from evil, many of us would dearly love to experience deliverance from our own incompetence, weakness, and failure, too. While we sense rather acutely that a spiritual battle rages for us and within us, we also feel disheartened by our inability to emulate the great heroes of the faith. As we look around at mature believers who seem so content, so godly, so patient, and so comparatively perfect, many of us would like to pass the tests and conquer sin with better results. Failing the tests creates great angst within us.

> *Many of us would dearly love to experience deliverance from our own incompetence, weakness, and failure.*

The book of Hebrews may help give some perspective at this point. It's a little shocking: Joseph and Samson in the same chapter (Hebrews 11) touted equally as heroes. Both appear as models of faith, but their lives contrast radically.

Joseph—a paragon of moral purity, flees the seductive advances of Potiphar's wife (Genesis 39–47).

Samson—a picture of moral laxity, resorts to prostitutes for company (Judges 13–16).

Joseph—a man of integrity and honesty, speaks the truth at all costs.

Samson—always ready to lie and deceive, to serve himself or save his skin.

Joseph—an example of forgiveness, even to those who have personally wounded him.

Samson—a portrait of vengeance and violence with complete strangers.

How could these Old Testament figures share the same stage? The shaggy Samson, wild-eyed and lonely, jilted and hunted, humiliated and abandoned, fails in every way. His wedding plans fell to pieces; his "friends" turned out to be double-crossing thieves; he battles loneliness; he falls from regional ruler to local prison inmate; and he dies under a pile of rubble after a horrific destruction. Samson represents virtually everything we would *not* want for our children. However, he gets specifically named among the faithful in Hebrews 11. His inclusion highlights at least two truths for our lives.

Faith does not protect us from failure.

First, faith does not protect us from failure. Samson's story defies the common teaching today that people with heroic-sized faith can routinely conquer disease, avoid disaster, and experience prosperity. Faith does not give us control of the universe, nor does it give us control of God.

Second, failure does not suggest a lack of faith. "If only I had more faith . . . I could have been healed; my marriage could have been saved; I would not have been bankrupted." Our failure to succeed in every venture of life has little to do with our level of faith.

Does the Father really measure our level of love or trust (faith) and hand out rewards accordingly? What sort of love is that?

Failure does not suggest a lack of faith.

Samson deserves his place in the Hall of Faith in Hebrews 11 not because he shines so brightly but because God shines brightly at the end of his life. Blinded, humiliated, shamed, and degraded, he calls out to the Lord for the strength to perform one last mighty feat. It's the only prayer of Samson's that the Bible records. And God in His grace hears and responds. Isn't that just like Him?

The biblical Hall of Fame describes the faith of men and women in the past, but also the great faithfulness of the Father throughout the ages. The only failure that ultimately matters is the failure to have faith.

Lead us not into testing, but deliver us from the evil.

Most people would describe Dr. Robert Wetzel as a Christian statesman. His career in higher education, training men and women for ministry, dates back to 1961, and he has served as president of a small seminary in Upper East Tennessee since 1991. He exudes gentleness and wisdom.

In 2007, I asked him and several other Christian college presidents for their number-one piece of advice for believers in our day and time. I expected Dr. Wetzel to ponder the question for several minutes. After all, he had a lifetime of experience and observation to distill into a single exhortation. But without a moment's hesitation, he replied:

> Pray every day, "Deliver us from evil." Lives are irrevocably changed by sin, and even with redemption, the scars and [the] pain continue. Do not compromise your Christian witness or forfeit your influence by letting Satan have the victory.[10]

As Jesus teaches us the Prayer, He addresses the fundamental flaw with which we all grapple. He raises the issues of testing and evil that confront us every day and He gives us great hope. Just when we may feel overwhelmed by our own faithlessness or sinfulness, Jesus reminds us to turn to the Father, the One who leads us through those valleys and delivers us from the evil.

Lead us not into testing, but deliver us from the evil. These two short statements become more than a cry of desperation. They reflect an affirmation of our desire to trust and obey.

CHAPTER 10

Yours Is the Kingdom, the Power, and the Glory

Abandoning Our Pursuit of Control and Fame

For yours is the kingdom, the power, and the glory forever.[1]

Power and glory. As Jesus uttered these words, His audience no doubt made associations that we do not. They had lived as the oppressed and powerless for generations. They had watched as soldiers, well-trained, well-equipped, but not well-meaning had ruthlessly subjugated their land. *Power.* The word had special meaning. It denoted something they'd lost and something feared by those common folk listening to Jesus on the hillside. They despised the tyrannical rule of Herod the tetrarch, the inflated taxation imposed by Rome, the threats and violence of the *pax Romana.* Peace of Rome? At best it felt like a coerced quiet; people forced into silence, driven into submission.

While most of Israel languished in poverty—laced with all the suspicion, fear, and division that accompany it—the powerful enjoyed the good life. Amphitheaters, hippodromes, palaces, shrines, fortifications, forums, and fountains all served the desires of the wealthy and the politically powerful. The irony of the word *power* was poignant to that hillside audience. They chafed under it every day. They despised it. They craved it. So when Jesus concludes the Prayer with the words "Yours [O, Father] is the kingdom, *the power, and the glory,*" His words ignited the hearts of His hearers. It probably felt like a call to insurrection.

Greater Than the Romans

Power and glory typified the Roman worldview. The Roman conquest of the known world reflected their insatiable thirst for power. The Roman machine was not fueled by religion or philosophy but by wealth, power, and the pursuit of glory. For religion, the Romans assimilated the Greek pantheon of their day and simply gave the Greek gods new names. Zeus became Jupiter, Poseidon became Neptune, Hades became Pluto, Athena became Minerva, Aphrodite became Venus, Artemis became Diana, and so on. The stories remained basically the same. Only the names changed, to give a thin Roman veneer. Such was their disinterest in religion and the gods. Similarly, they gave little attention to philosophy, whose main purpose in the ancient world was to moralize about how people should live. The Romans had minimal interest in such moralizing. It would interfere with their greed, lust, violence, and hedonism. Leave philosophy, mostly, to the Greeks.

But power and glory? Bring it on.

When soldiers returned to Rome victorious from their conquests, they would march through the streets to the accolades of the crowds. They dragged their prisoners of war in chains behind the procession, toward a destiny of either servitude or gladiatorial combat in the Coliseum. Power and glory. *Dunamis* and *doxa*.

In that first century environment, Jesus' words sounded seditious. His words clearly challenged the prevailing power brokers of His day. The kingdom, the power, and the glory all belong to the Father, irrespective of the intimidation, the threats, the brutalization, the oppression, and the random violence of the Roman juggernaut. It would not and could not successfully defy Him. Anyone who prayed this Prayer was reaffirming their confidence in the supremacy and sovereignty of God over all human institutions, governments, and empires. To speak of God's kingdom, power, and glory seriously confronted all personal ambition and nationalism in that day, and ours.

> *Anyone who prayed this Prayer was reaffirming their confidence in the supremacy and sovereignty of God over all human institutions, governments, and empires.*

The Ancient Trilogy

Some of those listening to this Prayer surely recognized the language of Psalm 24. Psalm 24 provides the triumphant closing to the renowned trilogy of Psalms 22–24. These three psalms tell something of the gospel story for each of us, but also had a special place in the liturgy and lives of the Jews who endured the Roman period.

Psalm 22 opens with the heartfelt cry:

My God, my God, why have you forsaken me? Why are you so far from saving me, so far from the words of my groaning? O my God, I cry out by day, but you do not answer, by night, and am not silent.

vv. 1–2

We recognize these words as one of Jesus' utterances on the cross, but every ordinary Jew in the days of Jesus felt these words deeply. And the verses that follow perfectly describe the suffering of most Jews in ancient Israel. Psalm 22 rose beyond being a religious text. It became a cry of the day.

Do not be far from me, for trouble is near and there is no one to help. Many bulls surround me; strong bulls of Bashan encircle me. Roaring lions tearing their prey open their mouths wide against me. I am poured out like water, and all my bones are out of joint. My heart has turned to wax; it has melted away within me. My strength is dried up like a potsherd, and my tongue sticks to the roof of my mouth; you lay me in the dust of death. Dogs have surrounded me; a band of evil men has encircled me, they have pierced my hands and my feet. I can count all my bones; people stare and gloat over me. They divide my garments among them and cast lots for my clothing. But you, O LORD, be not far off; O my Strength, come quickly to help me. Deliver my life from the sword, my precious life from the power of the dogs.

vv. 11–20

The "bulls of Bashan" and the "roaring lions" provide graphic images of violence and terror. But the label "dogs" (verses 16 and 20) evoked contempt, as is still true in the Middle East today, and the Jews reserved it (for the most part) for Gentiles and foreigners. The psalmist penned the perfect description of Roman aggression, a thousand years before it struck Israel.

Psalm 23 then breaks in. We may know the psalm best from funerals: "The LORD is my shepherd; I shall not want" (KJV). The desperation and deep pain of Psalm 22 gives way to a quiet confidence in Psalm 23.

Even though I walk through the valley of the shadow of death, I will fear no evil, for you are with me; your rod and your staff, they comfort me. You prepare a table before me in the presence of my enemies. You anoint my head with oil; my cup overflows. Surely goodness and love will follow me all the days of my life, and I will dwell in the house of the LORD forever.

vv. 4–6

Those days of Roman occupation, of disempowerment, and of helplessness marked a walk through the valley of the shadow of death, and for some Jews, into death itself. Yet despite the hardships, the Lord would supply the needs of His people. He would provide. His covenant love would not cease. And then Psalm 24 bursts forth.

In this triumphant psalm, death and destruction get swept off the stage. Center stage belongs to the King of glory. No longer will the people of God cry out for help. No longer shall they simply hang on in the midst of evil and perversity. Now they shall celebrate the vindication of their faith and the coming of the kingdom, power, and glory of the Lord.

> Lift up your heads, O you gates; be lifted up, you ancient doors, that the King of glory may come in. Who is this King of glory? The LORD strong and mighty, the LORD mighty in battle. Lift up your heads, O you gates; lift them up, you ancient doors, that the King of glory may come in. Who is he, this King of glory? The LORD Almighty—he is the King of glory.

vv. 7–10

Any of us who had been listening to Jesus teach the Prayer that day, would likely have recognized the core themes from these familiar psalms. Israel had clung to these prayers and hopes for centuries, and now Jesus reframes those ancient words with fresh, but equally stunning language. "Deliver us from the evil. For yours is the kingdom, the power, and the glory, forever!"

While our ears may have grown deaf to these nuances, we can at least see Jesus tying together the dreams and hopes of His hearers. When things look bleak, remember the ancient Word of the Lord. When hardship threatens to extinguish our hope, revisit the psalms that affirm our pain, then cast a vision for that day when joy shall be made complete. When fear and intimidation drive us into a bunker, recall the Lord "strong and mighty," the King of glory, who shall return.

The Prayer draws on the past (prophecy and psalm) to help us endure the present, with an eye on a glorious future. This closing phrase of the Prayer ties together the work of God in the world, yesterday, today, and forever.

> *The Prayer draws on the past to help us endure the present, with an eye on a glorious future.*

Power and Glory Today

Power and glory. Our minds quickly skip to people with enormous reserves of wealth or huge followings. Athletic superstars, international rock stars, high-profile politicians, and renowned actors all have power and glory. Bill Gates and Warren Buffett, because of their extraordinary wealth, have tremendous influence. Power and glory belong to the elite, the few, and the privileged.

However, we all take an interest in power and glory. Even those of us without two dollars in the bank, with no apparent influence and few achievements to point to, find ourselves drawn to these same pursuits.

Henri Nouwen described the three great temptations for *all* humanity as power, fame, and success. They lure us like bees to honey.

We spend much of our lives striving with power issues, struggling to either dominate others (which can lead to tyranny) or avoid domination by them (sometimes expressed in rebellion). This tension stays with many of us from adolescence to death. Additionally, something within us yearns for significance (just a form of fame). We want our lives to matter and count for something with others, perhaps many others. We work for recognition and appreciation, even if it's only those closest to us—parents, a spouse, a friend, a boss, our children. Finally, many of us vigorously pursue success, in part because it gives us power and fame.

Every day we wrestle these demons. These gargoyles leer at us from their lofty perches, though many of us find ourselves not so much afraid as seduced. Like the tempter of old (Genesis 3:4–5), inner voices coax us to desire personal power and glory. The call feels irresistible.

> *Our pursuit of power and glory inevitably produces conflict and discontent.*

It's not that we crave *lots* of power and glory, just a little; a little authority over others, a few accolades and bouquets. But the *little* quickly becomes insufficient and our lust for more becomes insatiable.

Our pursuit of power and glory inevitably produces conflict and discontent. Most of us discover that whenever we feed this longing, we nourish a cutworm. The cutworm, a soft-bodied caterpillar with a voracious appetite, can destroy a small garden plant very quickly, often cutting off its stem at ground level by chewing through it. Because it hides in the soil during the day, it can be hard to detect, except that the plant is obviously perishing. In the same way, our pursuit of power and glory finds easy camouflage in our culture, while steadily ravaging our lives.

The Prayer of Jesus slices straight to the core of such corruption: "For *yours* is the kingdom, the power, and the glory, forever."

Only as we relinquish our own pursuit of power and glory can we know the freedom of the kingdom and the richest blessings of the Lord's Prayer. True liberation comes when we surrender power and cease striving for it. Real release happens when we give up the dream of personal fame and glory. It's counterintuitive, but it's the kingdom way.

Those who knew Roy Weece described him first and foremost as a man of great humility. Indeed, his refusal to pursue personal power and glory magnified his effectiveness. Roy served as a college minister at the University of Missouri-Columbia for thirty-nine years. He did not wear trendy clothing or boast great knowledge about church growth or discipleship. He simply kept directing students to Christ and the Word of God (which he had lovingly memorized in enormous chunks). When he retired from college ministry in his late seventies (who says youth ministers should be under thirty?) his ministry still reached over five hundred students each semester. One former student who knew him made these observations:

He made it a point to share Jesus with at least three people each day of his life. I never heard sarcasm or vulgarity come out of his mouth. He took his students weekly to minister in the local women's correctional facility. I never heard about an argument between him and his wife, nor did I ever hear him joke about her. He valued his family above anything else in this life (besides Jesus). Now all of his children are in ministry.[2]

Roy passed away in April 2007. He left not just a well-oiled ministry machine. He left a legacy in the lives of his family and thousands of students, a legacy grounded in character not performance, humility not pride, cooperation not competition.

The competitive rivalry in marriages, churches, and workplaces makes it obvious that power and glory remain destructively attractive among us. We drop names of important people we've met or know. We casually mention how early we rise for prayer. We talk pridefully about our careers and promotions. We chat about our past successes and future projects. Each conversation offers another opportunity for us to exalt ourselves in the eyes of others. But Jesus casts a pall on our corrosive quest.

Our hearts find healing when we lay down our passion for power and give up our grasp for glory. How else shall we submit to one another (Ephesians 5:21) or practice piety in secret?

None of this comes naturally or easily. Perhaps all the more reason to hand it to the Father, as Jesus suggests. After all, only His power and glory matters ultimately.

"For *yours* is the kingdom, the power, and the glory, forever."

It's About Him

As Jesus draws His Prayer to a climax, He uses powerful language—the language of human history. Individuals and nations have wrestled since creation to build kingdoms, accumulate power, and receive glory. From the Pharaohs of Egypt to the Caesars of Rome and corporate executives today we see example after example of the human pursuit of greatness. But the Prayer challenges such a pursuit. We discover afresh that all of history is really God's story more than our own. It's about Him.

The Bible is not about how God fits into *our* story, but how we fit into *His*. Yet we often get it backwards.

> *The Bible is not about how God fits into* our *story, but how we fit into* His.

How often do we open the Scriptures to understand ourselves? We want God to clarify *our* lives, not highlight *His*.

Five principles for prosperity, three steps to healing, six truths for parenting, four keys to personal happiness. We scour the Book for timeless tips on marriage, family, friendship, and a settled soul. It's all about us, or so we think.

How does the Father want to bless us, use us, help us, heal us, guide us, and give to us? If we study the Book at all, it's often to get advice for our own issues—our needs, wants, and feelings. We analyze verses and chapters, looking for tidbits to teach or some private guidance for today. Genie in the bottle: God in the Bible.

However, the Bible is not a therapy textbook. It reveals God's story and relentlessly asserts that the main character of history is Christ. The Old Testament points to Him (see John 5:39; Galatians 3:24). The New Testament (Gospels and Epistles) reveals and explains Him. Even Revelation thrusts Him forward as the central figure for eternity:

> Then I heard what sounded like a great multitude, like the roar of rushing waters and like loud peals of thunder, shouting: "Hallelujah! For our Lord God Almighty reigns. Let us rejoice and be glad and give him glory! For the wedding of the Lamb has come, and his bride has made herself ready." . . . I saw heaven standing open and there before me was a white horse, whose rider is called Faithful and True. With justice he judges and makes war. His eyes are like blazing fire, and on his head are many crowns. He has a name written on him that no one knows but he himself. He is dressed in a robe dipped in blood, and his name is the Word of God. The armies of heaven were following him, riding on white horses and dressed in fine linen, white and clean. Out of his mouth comes a sharp sword with which to strike down the nations. "He will rule them with an iron scepter." He treads the winepress of the fury of the wrath of God Almighty. On his robe and on his thigh he has this name written: KING OF KINGS AND LORD OF LORDS.

> Revelation 19:6–7, 11–16

When we read, study, teach, or present Scripture, where do we begin? Have we too quickly and unconsciously elevated our own needs and self-importance, thinking that we play the leading role in the divine / human drama? The inspiration and preservation of Scripture means little if we merely manipulate it for ideas and insights into better lives.

Self-help books abound. We don't need another text to dispense common sense. We do, however, need a divine Word that opens our eyes to the cosmos and the extraordinary mystery of the Father—who He is, what He is doing, why He does it, and where He's taking it all.

The drama of the Word beckons us to join God's world, where He takes the initiative, has control, and determines the outcomes. And that is precisely what the Prayer affirms in this climactic statement. All of history is really His story not our story. The rise and fall of earthly kingdoms and nations seems inconsequential when we affirm that the only kingdom that matters is His, that all power ultimately rests in Him and all glory belongs to Him.

From Control to Surrender

None of us find it easy to release control of our lives. Yet this closing phrase of the Prayer beckons us to do just that. As we elevate His kingdom, power, and glory we naturally relegate our own. The ancient words of John the Baptizer come back to mind: "He must increase, but I must decrease" (John 3:30 NASB). We can't exalt ourselves and elevate the Father at the same time. We can't grip on to life tightly and yet trust Him with it simultaneously. We can't pursue our own glory and honor and also ascribe all dominion, power, and glory to Him. It just won't work. So we should consider the words of John the Baptizer very carefully. They ought not to simply roll off our tongues, especially for those of us who need control in our lives.

Control matters to us. We'd like to have control of our finances and our future, control of our homes and our health, control of our time and our careers. We struggle when the unexpected happens that spins these areas out of our control.

How will we cope when we don't have money to do all we'd like to do? What will we do when our children leave home and our protection (control) and branch out into the world on their own? Our lives feel driven by the "what ifs." We fear, deep down, that if we loosen our grip, everything just might collapse.

Our lives feel driven by the "what ifs."

This last phrase of the Prayer creates a tension for us if we pray it, and live it, earnestly. *Yours is the kingdom, the power, and the glory.* It confronts everything we believe and value, which is why we may applaud the midlife decision of many people to shift their ambition from success to significance. Even in the church we applaud this realignment of a life.

We usually define success as the achievement of power, fame, and wealth. In contrast, significance pursues personal influence. So we move from being wild-eyed entrepreneurs to being misty-eyed mentors. It all sounds very godly, and a big step toward the heart of the Prayer, but is it?

The journey from success to significance can become, for many of us, little more than changing roles in the same game: the shift from player to coach—no longer trying to throw the glorious touchdowns ourselves but calling the plays from the sidelines. Many coaches simply trade one pursuit of glory for another.

Significance is simply success by another name.

Various motives may propel our pursuit of significance (which can include great generosity of time and money)—disillusionment with material goals, a fresh vision for people, weariness with the drive to succeed, a sense of wanting broader influence—but the bottom line remains ominously static. We still want to affect and be affirmed by people. Success and significance build on the same foundation: our pride, self-belief, and self-importance.

Perhaps it's not changing roles in the game that marks our spiritual development, but changing games.

The Prayer insists, right down to this last phrase, on another option—surrender. We move forward most in our walk with God when we abandon both success and significance and embrace surrender. Surrender changes everything. Only genuine surrender turns subtle self-service into authentic God service. Only true surrender to the Lord frees us to do whatever He bids. And such surrender is countercultural to say the least.

When the apostle Paul declared, "I die daily" (1 Corinthians 15:31 NASB), he did not seek to impress his readers with his own sacrificial efforts. He affirmed the centrality of surrender for all of us and the truth of Jesus' words that "unless a kernel of wheat falls to the ground and dies, it remains only a single seed. But if it dies, it produces many seeds" (John 12:24).

As beloved followers of Christ, we surrender daily and fully to God's kingdom, power, and glory. And He takes our lives—what we have and what we lack—and accomplishes His purposes.

In the eighteenth century, the French Jesuit Jean-Pierre de Caussade wrote: "Without divine action, everything is nothing, with it nothing is everything."[3]

Full and unconditional surrender to God can sound utterly barren and empty. We may see nothing in it—no power and glory for us at all. But with His action, that nothing becomes everything. Our resistance to surrender and insistence on our agenda may produce crowds, fame, and influence that others envy, but without His action it proves vain. And He achieves nothing of deep spiritual consequence in or through us.

Yours is the kingdom, the power, and the glory forever.

The journey to freedom requires the relinquishment of our personal pursuit of power and glory. As we pray this phrase it reminds us that the Father calls us to surrender our control and trust in His care. We join His story and resolve to give Him glory—forever.

CHAPTER 11

Amen

Living With a Yes

Amen.

> Some words resist translation. We don't translate *Amen*.
> We don't translate *Hallelujah*. We don't translate *Hosanna*.
> These words accumulate layers of meanings through the
> centuries and radiate rich associations and connections.
> When we translate them they fall flat.[1]

We utter the "untranslatable" *Amen* with regularity and it
serves several purposes. It commonly signifies the formal end
of our prayer, a sort of "I'm done." It lets hearers know that
we've concluded our address to God. Additionally, in some congregations the audience punctuates the preaching with various
Amens, soft and gentle whispers as well as loud and energetic
exclamations. In this context, the term generally means "I agree.

Good word! Yes, I'm with you on that." But perhaps we have overlooked the most profound elements of this simple term.

From a biblical perspective the *Amen* has great significance. When the writers of the New Testament concluded a written prayer with *Amen,* they intended the word to evoke far more than "next item on the agenda." At the very least, it declared a powerful and confident *Yes* to the Father. Paul, Peter, and Jude (for example) close some of their prayers with this short no-nonsense word.

> The Lord will rescue me from every evil attack and will bring me safely to his heavenly kingdom. To him be glory for ever and ever. *Amen.*
>
> 2 Timothy 4:18

> May the God of peace . . . work in us what is pleasing to him, through Jesus Christ, to whom be glory for ever and ever. *Amen.*
>
> Hebrews 13:20–21

> So that in all things God may be praised through Jesus Christ. To him be the glory and the power for ever and ever. *Amen.*
>
> 1 Peter 4:11

> To the only God our Savior be glory, majesty, power and authority, through Jesus Christ our Lord, before all ages, now and forevermore! *Amen.*
>
> Jude 25

Each of these prayers finishes with a flourish—to God be the glory—and the *Amen* stands as the definitive exclamation mark. Then in Revelation, the apostle John details a heavenly vision in which four living creatures and twenty-four elders fall down before the Lamb (Jesus). Each creature and elder has a harp and a golden bowl of incense "which are the prayers of the saints" (Revelation 5:8). They begin, in unison, to sing a new song of worship and praise to the Lamb. Gradually, myriads upon myriads of angels join in the song and the momentum builds. Imagine the volume and intensity growing by the moment as the heavenly choristers hear the song swelling and hurl themselves into it like the wave spreading around a baseball stadium. Finally, in a burst of energy, "every creature in heaven and on earth and under the earth and on the sea, and all that is in them" join the song: "To him who sits on the throne and to the Lamb be praise and honor and glory and power, for ever and ever!" (Revelation 5:13).

Not a living creature wants to miss this glorious moment. Since Golgotha, all of creation has waited with restraint for this moment. Now the Lamb that was slain—the Lord Jesus—stands front and center, ready to fulfill the redemptive plan of God. And as all of creation joins this flourishing anthem, "the four living creatures said, '*Amen*,' and the elders fell down and worshiped" (Revelation 5:14).

In the splendor and spectacle of the moment, have the creatures been rendered speechless by this scene of unadulterated praise and adoration? Do they fumble for a word—any word—and only manage to squeeze out a simple *Amen?* Not for a moment. In fact, they find the most appropriate word of all to declare—*Yes*.

This inconspicuous Hebrew word carries enormous history, depth, and force. In much the same way that *Shalom* in Hebrew (used when Jews greet or part) means far more than simply "peace," so *Amen* captures the assurance of the soul. It expresses acknowledgment, agreement, commitment, and confidence. No Greek word conveyed the same range of nuances, so the early church simply carried this Hebrew term into their daily vocabulary. Early efforts to find Greek synonyms such as *aleuthinos* ("that which is not false") and *genoito* ("would that it were so") proved altogether inadequate.[2] These pale alternatives were like skim milk options to the full cream of *Amen. Amen* said it best.

> Amen *said it best.*

Eugene Peterson writes:

> We come to God with a history of nay-saying, of rejecting and being rejected. At the throne of God we are immersed in God's yes, a yes that silences all our noes and calls forth an answering yes in us. . . . Amen! Amen is recurrent and emphatic among God's people. It is robust and exuberant. There is nothing cowering, cautious, or timid in it. It is an answering word, purged of all negatives. . . . When we Christians say or sing or shout, "amen," God hears our unequivocating assent to his irrevocable Yes to us, the Yes of our redeemer Lamb, the Yes of our creator King.[3]

When we begin to grasp the magnitude of this yes, we understand why Jesus finished the Prayer with it.[4] Could there be a more positive, more compelling, or more vision-filled word? In the midst of our world of negativity, we reach out prayerfully to the One who says Yes to us. And having laid our lives entirely before Him through the phrases of the Prayer, we conclude with perhaps the greatest word of faith that the early church could muster—*Amen.* Yes. And this word morphs into a core value by which we choose to live.

Choosing to Live in the Yes

The optimist declares the glass is half full; the pessimist bemoans that it stands half empty; and the engineer concludes that the glass is twice the size it needs to be. We all look at life through different lenses. Some of us live on the edge, always taking risks and savoring new challenges. Others of us prefer caution and planning, stability and predictability. Some of us enjoy constant crowds and much laughter. Others of us find energy in solitude and reflection. Our personalities vary enormously, as do our preferences. And we do well to realize that God ordains this diversity, placing no greater premium on one view of the glass over another.

Yet irrespective of the window through which we see life, the Prayer calls each of us to live in the *Yes*.

Amen—the *Yes*-word—might seem like the domain of positive thinkers. Surely it justifies their life approach more than any other. We might excuse everyone who concludes that this powerful Yes belongs to just a few—the salesmen, the visionar-ies, the enthusiasts, the motivators, and the energetic. *Amen* surely belongs to them. They exude the Yes. They see all of life as fantastic, wonderful, incredible, and full of potential. They deserve the Yes-word because they refuse to accept No in their lives.

But the *Amen* runs much deeper than the smiles, backslaps, cheers, whoops, and hype of the few. It belongs to all of us. It calls each of us to live by faith, not faith in our circumstances, that everything will be fine, but faith in the One who controls our lives and eternity. *Amen* refuses to let us live in the waist-deep No of our lives. *Amen* calls us to lift our eyes beyond the horizon and step forth with renewed confidence.

This Yes emerges not from a vain sense of invincibility or an egotistical dose of self-confidence but from a deep trust in the Lord's grace and provision. The Yes derives from a settled place where the waters run still and deep within us. It reflects roots that reach into our soul, not a hard shell that can deflect the bumps.

Helen Roseveare served Christ in Congo/Zaire in the mid-twentieth century. As a medical doctor, she felt called to help establish a hospital for the sick and the suffering in that land but found herself trapped there during the terrible Congolese uprising of the 1960s. One day the rebels came to the com-pound where she lived and forced her and many others out into the jungle at gunpoint. During her five months in captivity she suffered abuse, mistreatment, violence, and deprivation at their hands. On October 29, 1964, a rebel lieutenant pressed a gun to her forehead, cursed her, and threatened to kill her. At that moment, Hugh, a seventeen-year-old student who had been abducted with Helen, threw himself between her and the rebel lieutenant. The rebels beat Hugh savagely and kicked his near lifeless body out of the way.

Helen later wrote:

> If I had prayed any prayer, it would have been: "My God, my God, why hast Thou forsaken me?"

> Then, quietly, God met with me. He reminded me that twenty years before I had asked for the privilege of being a missionary. "This is it. Don't you want it?" He seemed to say to me.

> *The fantastic privilege of being identified with our Saviour dawned afresh in my heart.*

> He had asked me for the loan of my body. He had not taken away the pain or the cruelty or the humiliation. No, it had still been there, all there, yet it suddenly became quite different. In the depth of my weakness, He revealed His strength. It was now—with Him, in Him, for Him. It had been triumphant victory in the midst of apparent defeat. Joy had come for tears. *Privilege had displaced all sense of cost.*[5]

> *As we hear afresh the Lord's unequivocal Yes to us, we discover new levels of courage and hope, even amidst pain and despair.*

Living in the Yes does not turn us into Pollyanna look-alikes on a mission to cheer up the world. As we hear afresh the Lord's unequivocal Yes to us, we discover new levels of courage and hope, even amidst pain and despair. We find our tears mingled with peace, our fears gently eased by His presence, and our deepest heartaches soothed by faith. While those around us declare *No,* the Lord says *Yes* (*Amen*). *Yes*—we belong to Him. *Yes*—He cares for us. *Yes*—He guards our soul. *Yes*—He secures eternity and prepares a place for us. *Yes. Yes. Yes.* And we live in that *Amen.*

The *Amen,* however, extends beyond affirmation and incorporates truth.

Living in Truth

Nothing speaks to truth like the *Amen.* Earlier in the Sermon on the Mount, Jesus admonished His hearers to quit making oaths by heaven, by earth, by Jerusalem, or even by their own heads. "Simply let your 'Yes' be 'Yes,' and your 'No,' 'No'; anything beyond this comes from the evil one" (Matthew 5:37).

International politics is infamous for its careful nuancing of words, leaving ambiguity and loopholes in as many places as possible. The days of straightforward speech seem long gone. A handshake is worth little and a signature not much more. But the kingdom of God functions differently.

The kingdom that we have prayed might come refuses to equivocate or manipulate. Truth defines the kingdom way, which makes *Amen* one of the core kingdom words. It takes on almost covenant quality when we speak it to each other. When the word stands alone, it assumes contractual overtones. Can you imagine someone crying out, "A partial *Amen* to that!

Amen to that statement, but with the following objections and exceptions!" The exclamation is definitive, decisive, complete. When we utter such a declaration, we accept an obligation because it affirms what we believe to be most true, and as followers of Jesus we bind ourselves to the truth.

The apostle John found the perfect epithet with which to describe Jesus: "Full of grace and truth" (John 1:14, 17). And in that summation of the life and ministry of Jesus, John laid out part of the blueprint for the body of Christ—full of grace and truth. No compromise.

This little word—*Amen*—reminds us that the little things count.

> *We must not reserve the* Amen *for big issues or serious moments.*

In September 2004, the $260 million space probe Genesis returned to Earth after a three-year voyage. It carried billions of atoms collected from solar wind, the first cosmic samples to be returned to Earth from beyond the moon. But the 450-pound capsule's parachutes never deployed, and it slammed into the Utah desert at nearly two hundred miles per hour.

After an investigation, NASA officials found the cause. Four pencil-stub-size gravity switches, designed to trigger release of the parachutes, were *installed backwards*.[6]

The little things count.

We prefer to talk about "the big picture" or "the things that really matter." For example, why fuss over a white lie or a little gossip when we could crusade against world hunger or abortion? As believers, we're sometimes inclined to dismiss the little things—but the devil can be in the details.

In 1811, Hannah More wrote, "Does the habit of loose talking or allowed exaggeration never lead to falsehood, never move into deceit?"[7] In essence, she understood that we must not reserve the *Amen* for big issues or serious moments. It stands as a life word for application to every context—the check-out at the grocery store, the church parking lot, the work lunchroom, everywhere. As we live in God's *Yes* to us and affirm our *Yes* to Him, we choose to make *Yes* our guiding principle with others, too.

We choose to live in the truth at all times, knowing that small practices (for good or ill) can become regular habits. No longer shall we put a spin on our "success," twist statistics, or exaggerate the facts to impress someone. The children of such language are always falsehood and deception.

Isn't this much ado about nothing? Just as we start to think so, an *Amen* fires across the bow of such indifference. *Yes*—truth—begins our walk with God and concludes every statement and conversation we have with each other.

Hannah More continued, "Before we positively determine that small faults are innocent, we must try to prove that they shall never outgrow their primitive dimensions. We must make certain that the infant shall never become a giant."[8]

The little things count. It matters that as believers we practice the smaller virtues. Likewise, it matters that we avoid scrupulously the lesser sins. Integrity does not mean *fairly reliable.* It implies *utter consistency.* Godliness means dedication to purity and truth in the smallest of matters.

Hidden habits hurt us, however small, and nothing hurts us more than a broken word—the violated *Amen.* So we avoid the white lies, the careless exaggeration, the meaningless promises, and the blatant deception.

It won't matter that we have booster rockets, high-tech disks, and phenomenal programming if our "little switches"— governed by that little kingdom word *Amen*—fail us. If we dismiss the details, we diminish our spiritual formation. Deeds, not our dreams, determine our character. Godliness is not a claim we make but a lifestyle we demonstrate—not with bursts of brilliance but with steady attention to our word, the word, *Amen.*

Beyond the Critical Spirit

Amen. This ancient word also challenges our human practice of nay-saying. All too often the No rises up within us and against us, or we blurt it out against others. We receive and dish out truckloads of criticism. Indeed, some people, not particularly well-meaning, make it *their* mission in life to negate *our* mission in life. "You can't do that! No! Don't bother trying! Who do you think you are? You're incompetent. Get someone else to do it." Every effort we make receives critical assessment rather than encouragement. Every

> *This ancient word also challenges our human practice of nay-saying.*

positive word we receive is overwhelmed by the waves of negative words that crash over us.

The phenomenon is not new. John Calvin, in the sixteenth century wrote, "If others have any vices, we are not content to criticize them sharply and severely, but we exaggerate them hatefully."[9]

The Australian culture calls this the tall-poppy syndrome. The phrase refers to the practice of putting down anyone who succeeds or does well. As they grow above the rest of the field, their stalks are cut from below to reduce their stature. This social surgery supposedly maintains a level of equality and humility, but forced humility is no humility at all. We call it humiliation.

In contrast, *Amen* is the word of affirmation not criticism. And it seems that until we hear this word echoing deep within our own hearts, we struggle to express it to others. Our own beaten spirits make a poor launch pad for nurturing others. Thus only as we begin to live in the *Yes* can we allow others to do the same.

We walk some fine lines. In education we speak positively of critical thinking. Teachers want their students to assess and evaluate a problem or a piece of writing from various perspectives. Critical thinking often guides us to constructive change and helpful improvements. As we identify problems and isolate glitches in systems, we can fix them. But how do we handle the blurred line between critical thinking and a critical spirit? Critical *thinking* at its best displays gentleness, analysis, thoughtfulness, and constructiveness. The critical *spirit* at its worst is close-minded, intolerant, aggressive, and destructive. When we genuinely live in the *Amen* we find little room for the latter.

Jesus models this lifestyle. The only people whom He openly criticized were those who reserved the strongest Yes for themselves and took a perverted pleasure in pronouncing a strong No on everyone else. The Yes that the Pharisees lived in was a Yes for themselves and of their own mak-ing. But Jesus constantly affirmed the beaten, the broken, and the burned-out. He spoke tenderly to a bent over and unattractive woman (Luke 13:11–12), to a tax collector who climbed a tree to see Him (Luke 19:2–5), to an outcast leper who appealed to Him (Mark 1:40–41), to a blind beggar who cried out to Him (Mark 10:46–52). These people, victims of the critical spirit of their age, crushed in spirit, drained of hope, shamed by their circumstances, rejected by the mainstream—these who lived in a world of constant no's—received grace from Christ.

> *Jesus constantly affirmed the beaten, the broken, and the burned-out.*

Was He blind to their conditions, to their sins, or to their failures? Could He not see their unworthiness, their unattractiveness, their neediness? Did He not realize that these were the outcasts, the rejects, the marginalized, the unproductive? They had nothing, gave nothing, and deserved nothing, but Jesus lived in the *Yes* and sought to draw others into that same place. A critical spirit would undermine such a mission.

The Spirit of the Lord is on me, because he has anointed me to preach good news to the poor. He has sent me to proclaim freedom for the prisoners and recovery of sight for the blind, to release the oppressed, to proclaim the year of the Lord's favor.

Luke 4:18–19

Any choice we make to embrace a critical spirit is a choice to oppose the mission of Christ. If the bedrock of the kingdom lies in the *Amen,* and it does, then our harsh assessment or unkind gossip about others serves to undermine the kingdom.

Does the *Amen* limit our capacity to call sin what it is? Not at all. Holiness demands that we pursue righteousness. We pray also to be delivered from evil. We can and must call evil by its name and be clear in our moral stance. The *Amen* does not silence us. On the contrary, it opens our mouths to speak new words, creative words, constructive words in the midst of the devastation of sin. The *Amen* empowers us to weep over the brokenness but hold the pieces together with grace; to grieve over fallenness but seek to restore, not destroy, the person. We oppose violence and abuse and speak a new way—the kingdom way.

The critical spirit denies the image of God in those around us. It sees only the negative residue of sin in others and exposes the negative residue of sin within our own lives. What better way to combat such shortsightedness than to embrace the *Amen*—the last word of the Prayer, the first word of our lives.

Importantly, this *Amen* is not just a word but a Person.

Not Just a Word but a Person

John of the Apocalypse gave Jesus the title *Amen:* "These are the words of *the Amen,* the faithful and true witness, the ruler of God's creation" (Revelation 3:14).

Suddenly *Amen* rises above a simple expiration of our breath or a short syllable we might utter. The *Amen* is a Person. This word becomes a title for Christ throughout eternity. This term points us not only to a concept but to the Savior.

John makes all the connections we've already observed—connections to faithfulness, integrity, truth, and the creative power of our word. And the title surprises us. Yet it drives home once again that Christianity is not a moral code to live by but a Person to live with and for; not a philosophical system or a collection of positive ideas but a Lord who embodies it all.

John shared rich company in this assessment. The apostle Paul understood it perfectly well. Writing to the Corinthians, he declared, "All the promises of God in Him are Yes, and in Him Amen, to the glory of God through us" (2 Corinthians 1:20 NKJV).

Amen cannot be reduced to four letters—*a-m-e-n*—in consecutive order, nor can it be captured entirely in a short dictionary definition. The word does not confine itself to a prayer closure or an exclamation to encourage the speaker. It finds its ultimate expression in the Person of Jesus. The One who whispers *Amen* in our ear—"Yes, you are my child"—as we come to saving faith. The One who boldly calls *Amen* to us over the cacophonous no's that assault us every day, if we'll but hear Him. The One who reserves the ultimate *Amen* for that moment we stand before God for eternity.

All the promises of God find their *Yes* in Christ. Everything good and true and beautiful that the Father has wanted to extend to us and to the world is caught up in Jesus. Christ fulfills every Yes that the Father has planned for us from eter-

> *All the promises of God find their Yes in Christ.*

nity. Little wonder that the angel of God would announce to the Laodicean church that Jesus is the *Amen*. The congregation that had drifted from Yes to Maybe, the believers who had abandoned God's Yes to embrace their own self-sufficiency, are invited to say Yes to Him again.

"Here I am! I stand at the door and knock. If anyone hears my voice and opens the door, I will come in and eat with him, and he with me" (Revelation 3:20).

What more fitting way for Jesus to conclude the Prayer than to reveal His own eternal name? What more appropriate way for us to live the Lord's Prayer than to open the door and invite Him in to share every meal with us?

Postscript

The Lord's Prayer represents the deepest commitment of the human life imaginable. Frank Laubach put it this way:

> [The Lord's Prayer] is the prayer most used and least understood. People think they are asking God for something. They are not—they are offering God something. . . . The Lord's Prayer is not a prayer to God to do something we want done. It is more nearly God's prayer to us, to help Him do what He wants done. . . . The Lord's Prayer is not intercession. It is enlistment.[1]

We come to the end of the book, but just the next step on the Journey. So much lies ahead. We started in the Introduction with a definition of spiritual formation: *The process of being with Christ in order to become like Christ and consequently live for Christ.* Every element of the Prayer has addressed this definition in one way or another and finds its fulfillment and perfect example in Christ.

Truly the Prayer expresses a lifestyle, not just a vocabulary. It captures all of the major themes that our Christian spiritual guides have suggested throughout the centuries. It draws us into the family of God and the community of believers. It motivates a pursuit of holiness and the surrender of our own kingdoms. As our hearts grow more willing for the things of God, we find ourselves looking more to Him for everything every day and desiring to share His blessings with the impoverished. As grace comes to us and pours through us we discover its radical power. And as we hold fast to faith in testing times and develop the discipline of resisting evil through confession and repentance, we experience life to the full.

We don't pray the Prayer to solicit God's attention. We pray it to catch our own. In a world buried in the malaise of mediocrity, waist-deep in complacency, and swamped by our self-centeredness, the Prayer calls us to transformation. And as our lives conform to the plan and design of the Father, we discover that in giving everything we lose nothing. We prove true the words of Henri Nouwen: "We begin to perceive that the downward road [of releasing our own agenda and ambition] is not the road to hell, but the road to heaven."[2] The Prayer guides us step-by-step into practical expressions of Jesus' enigmatic teaching: "Whoever loses his life for my sake shall find it" (Matthew 10:39).

As you live the Prayer may you know the unfolding joy of His presence and the wonder of His transforming power.

Additional Resources

For additional resources related to this book, please visit *www.growingdeeper.com*.

You'll find the following available:

- Twelve-week small-group study guide

- Related book recommendations (annotated bibliography)

- Opportunity to receive (FREE) a regular e-zine that further explores the themes of the book

- Contact information if you'd like David Timms to speak on these topics at a meeting or retreat

═══ Selected Bibliography ═══

Allison, Dale C. *The Sermon on the Mount: Inspiring the Moral Imagination.* New York: Crossroad, 1999.

Banks, Robert. *Paul's Idea of Community.* Peabody, MA: Hendrickson, 1994.

Benner, David. *Surrender to Love.* Downers Grove, IL: InterVarsity, 2003.

Bonhoeffer, Dietrich. *Life Together.* Trans., John Doberstein. San Francisco: Harper & Row, 1954.

Bridges, Jerry. *The Pursuit of Holiness.* Colorado Springs: NavPress, 1982.

Calvin, John. *Golden Booklet of the True Christian Life.* Trans., Henry J. Van Andel. Grand Rapids, MI: Baker Books, 2005.

Carl, William J. *The Lord's Prayer for Today.* Louisville, KY: Westminster, 2006.

Carson, D.A. *The Sermon on the Mount.* Carlisle, UK: Paternoster, 1994.

Dodd, C.H. *The Parables of the Kingdom*. New York: Scribner's, 1958.

Foster, Richard, and James Bryan Smith. *Devotional Classics*. New York: HarperCollins, 1993.

Foster, Richard, and Emilie Griffin. *Spiritual Classics*. New York: HarperCollins, 2000.

Hernandez, Wil. *Henri Nouwen: A Spirituality of Imperfection*. Mahwah, NJ: Paulist, 2006.

Kelly, Thomas. *A Testament of Devotion*. New York: Harper-Collins, 1992.

Kempis, Thomas à. *The Imitation of Christ*. Trans., William C. Creasy. Notre Dame, IN: Ave Maria, 2001.

Laubach, Frank. *Letters by a Modern Mystic*. New York: New Readers Press, 1955.

_____. "Meditation on the Lord's Prayer." In *Man of Prayer*. Ed., Karen R. Norton. Syracuse, NY: Laubach Literacy Foundation, 1990, 325–26.

Law, William. *A Serious Call to a Devout and Holy Life*. New York: Random House, 2002.

Luthi, Walter, and Robert Brunner. *The Sermon on the Mount*. Edinburgh, UK: Oliver & Boyd, 1963.

Main, John. *Word Into Silence*. New York: Continuum International Publishing, 1980.

Manning, Brennan. *Ruthless Trust: The Ragamuffin's Path to God.* New York: HarperCollins, 2000.

Morrison, George. *Classic Sermons on the Lord's Prayer.* Ed., Warren Wiersbe. Grand Rapids, MI: Kregel, 2000.

Nouwen, Henri. "From Solitude to Community to Ministry." *Leadership.* Spring 1995.

_____. *Adam: God's Beloved.* Maryknoll, NY: Orbis, 1997.

_____. *The Selfless Way of Christ.* Maryknoll, NY: Orbis, 2007.

Palmer, Parker. *To Know As We Are Known.* San Francisco: HarperSanFrancisco, 1983.

Peterson, Eugene. *Reversed Thunder.* San Francisco: Harper & Row, 1988.

_____. *Eat This Book: A Conversation in the Art of Spiritual Reading.* Grand Rapids, MI: Eerdmans, 2006.

_____. *The Jesus Way.* Grand Rapids, MI: Eerdmans, 2007.

Roseveare, Helen. *Living Sacrifice.* London, UK: Hodder & Stoughton, 1979.

Taylor, Barbara Brown. *When God Is Silent.* Cambridge, MA: Cowley, 1998.

Timms, David. "Laws and Lies." *The LOOKOUT.* July 3, 2005.

_____. "Presidents . . . About Life." *The LOOKOUT.* January 6, 2008.

Tournier, Paul. *Guilt and Grace.* New York: Hodder & Stoughton, 1962.

Tozer, A.W. *The Pursuit of God.* Camp Hill, PA: Christian, 1982.

Willard, Dallas. *The Divine Conspiracy.* San Francisco: HarperCollins, 1998.

Willimon, William, and Stanley Hauerwas. *Lord, Teach Us.* Nashville: Abingdon, 1996.

Wright, N.T. *The Lord and His Prayer.* Grand Rapids, MI: Eerdmans, 1996.

Endnotes

Introduction

1. Information for this recounting of the story comes from two sites: "Douglas Mawson," Wikipedia, *http://en.wikipedia.org/wiki/ Douglas_Mawson,* and "The Ice Zone," *Outside Magazine, http:// outside.away.com/outside/features/200409/top_survival_stories_2. html.*

2. Benedict (c. 480–547) spent some years as a desert hermit, then founded twelve communities for monks, the best known of which is his first monastery at Monte Cassino in the mountains of southern Italy. The Rule of St. Benedict became one of the most influential religious rules in Western Christendom. Consequently, Benedict is often called the founder of Western Christian monasticism.

3. Bernard of Clairvaux (1090–1153) was a French abbot and the primary builder of the Cistercian monastic order.

4. Julian of Norwich (c. 1342–1416) is considered one of the greatest English mystics. We know little of her life aside from her writings. Even her name is uncertain, the name "Julian" coming from the Church of St. Julian where she lived in seclusion.

5. Catherine of Sienna (1347–1380) came from Sienna, Italy. At the age of seven she consecrated herself to Christ despite her

family's opposition. When she turned eighteen, she joined the Dominican Order and dedicated her life to helping the ill and the poor, whom she cared for in hospitals and homes. She died at thirty-three years of age.

6. St. John of the Cross (1542–1591), a Spanish mystic, worked with Saint Teresa of Avila in the reformation of the Carmelite order. His poetry and writings represent the summit of mystical Spanish literature and one of the peaks of all Spanish literature. He is one of the thirty-three Doctors of the Roman Catholic Church.

7. Teresa of Avila (1515–1582), a contemporary of St. John of the Cross and a Spanish mystic, toiled to reform the Carmelite order throughout her lengthy life. Roman Catholics recognize her as one of the thirty-three Doctors of the church, being one of only three women awarded the honor.

8. Madam Guyon (1648–1717), a French mystic, was imprisoned by the Roman Catholic Church, from 1695 to 1703, after publishing a book entitled *A Short and Easy Method of Prayer*. The church banned and burned her book but copies remained, because it is still in print today, encouraging believers to listen attentively to God as they read the Scriptures for themselves.

9. John Wesley (1703–1791), an early leader in the Methodist movement in England, emphasized "Christian perfection," or holiness of heart and life. Wesley traveled constantly, generally on horseback, preaching two or three times a day. He formed societies, opened chapels, and administered various aid charities in addition to being married and having nineteen children.

10. Dietrich Bonhoeffer (1906–1945) wore many hats: a German Lutheran pastor, theologian, participant in the German Resistance movement against Nazism, and a founding member of the Confessing Church. German authorities eventually implicated

him in a plot to assassinate Adolf Hitler. They arrested him in 1943, imprisoned him, and eventually hanged him just before the end of World War II.

11. Thomas Merton (1915–1968), one of the most influential Roman Catholic authors of the twentieth century and a Trappist monk based in Kentucky, was an acclaimed spiritual author, poet, and social activist.

12. Henri Nouwen (1932–1996), a Dutch Catholic priest who spent most of his life in the U.S., authored forty books on the spiritual life, read widely today by Protestants and Catholics alike. He spent the last ten years of his life living and sharing with mentally handicapped people at the L'Arche community of Daybreak in Toronto, Canada.

13. I base this count on the Greek text in Matthew 6:9–13 and include the familiar variant at the end ("for yours is the kingdom, and the power, and the glory to the ages. Amen.").

14. Barbara Brown Taylor, *When God Is Silent* (Cambridge, MA: Cowley, 1998), 50.

15. Wil Hernandez, *Henri Nouwen: A Spirituality of Imperfection* (Mahwah, NJ: Paulist, 2006), 32.

Chapter 1

1. John Grisham, *A Painted House* (New York: Bantam Dell, 2003), 1.

2. Charles Dickens, *A Tale of Two Cities,* ed., Richard Maxwell (New York: Penguin Classics, 2003), 1.

3. Shankar Vedantam, "Social Isolation Growing in U.S., Study Says," *Washington Post,* June 23, 2006, *www.washingtonpost.com/ wp-dyn/content/article/2006/06/22/AR2006062201763.html.*

4. Dietrich Bonhoeffer, *Life Together,* trans., John Doberstein (San Francisco: Harper & Row, 1954), 77–78.

5. Arthur Vermeersch, "Religious Profession," The Catholic Encyclopedia, *www.newadvent.org/cathen/12451b.htm*.

6. "General Mobility by Region, Sex and Age: 2005 to 2006," U.S. Census Bureau, *www.census.gov/population/www/socdemo/migrate/cps2006.html*.

7. David Benner, *Surrender to Love* (Downers Grove, IL: InterVarsity, 2003), 13.

8. Shane Hipps, *The Hidden Power of Electronic Culture* (Grand Rapids, MI: Zondervan, 2005), 111.

9. The word order of the Greek text actually begins with the word *Father* and reads, in order, "Father ours, the one (who is) in the heavens. . . ."

10. Many people associate the term *mantra* with Hinduism or New Age practices. However, the idea of a repeated word or phrase has a long and meaningful history in the church. For a helpful discussion, see John Main, *Word Into Silence* (New York: Continuum International Publishing, 1980), 49–64.

11. Parker Palmer, *To Know As We Are Known* (San Francisco: HarperSanFrancisco, 1983), 57.

Chapter 2

1. "Homelessness Statistics and Data," Substance Abuse and Mental Health Services Administration, *www.samhsa.gov/Matrix/statistics_homeless.aspx*.

2. "Top 50 Cities in the U.S. by Population and Rank," Infoplease, *www.infoplease.com/ipa/A0763098.html*.

3. "Statistics on Homeless Children & Youth," Macomb Intermediate School District, *www.misd.net/Homeless/statistics.htm*.

4. "Domestic Violence in the Workplace Statistics," American Institute on Domestic Violence, *www.aidv-usa.com/Statistics.htm*.

5. "The Facts on Domestic Violence," Family Violence Prevention Fund, *www.endabuse.org/resources/facts/DomesticViolence.pdf.*

6. Robert Putnam, *Bowling Alone: The Collapse and Revival of American Community* (New York: Simon & Schuster, 2001).

7. N. T. Wright, *The Lord and His Prayer* (Grand Rapids, MI: Eerdmans, 1996), 14–15. Note that the Jewish reluctance to speak the personal name of God also impacts their writing of His name. They prefer YHWH (without inserting vowels) to Yahweh, so that people think twice before attempting to pronounce it. Our old English word *Jehovah* is simply another guess at how those four letters could be made pronounceable.

8. I develop these ideas more in my article "Laws and Lies," *The LOOKOUT* (July 3, 2005), 4–5.

9. Henri Nouwen, "From Solitude to Community to Ministry," *Leadership* (Spring 1995).

10. Robert Banks, *Paul's Idea of Community* (Peabody, MA: Hendrickson, 1994), 49.

Chapter 3

1. William Willimon and Stanley Hauerwas, *Lord, Teach Us* (Nashville: Abingdon, 1996), 34.

2. Thomas Kelly, *A Testament of Devotion* (New York: HarperCollins, 1992), 10.

3. You can easily access phenomenal photographs of the universe at Jet Propulsion Laboratory, *www.jpl.nasa.gov.*

4. For a brief discussion affirming this view, see Douglas Ward, "The Third Heaven," The Voice, *www.cresourcei.org/thirdheaven.html.*

5. In the thirty-two instances, every occurrence incorporates the plural "kingdom *of the heavens.*" Matthew clearly wants to make a specific point about the comprehensive rulership of God at all

heavenly levels as the Jews understood them, including the very air that surrounds our present existence.

6. C. H. Dodd, *The Parables of the Kingdom* (New York: Scribner's, 1958), 34.

7. Dallas Willard, *The Divine Conspiracy* (San Francisco: HarperCollins, 1998), 73.

8. For example, 1:23; 3:9, 16; 4:3-4, 6-7, 10.

9. Based on the *New International Version,* Matthew uses the word *heavens* or *heavenly* seventy-seven times—more than the other three Gospel writers combined; Mark uses the terms fifteen times; Luke uses them twenty-nine times; John uses them eighteen times.

10. Matthew uses the phrase *Father in the heavens* eleven times throughout his gospel, and *heavenly Father* another seven times. For "Father in the heavens" see 5:16, 45; 6:1, 9; 7:11; 10:32–33; 12:50; 16:17; 18:14, 19. For "heavenly Father" see 5:48; 6:14, 26, 32; 15:13; 18:35; 23:9. Note the preponderance of instances in the Sermon on the Mount (Matthew 5–7), which accounts for nine of eighteen occurrences.

11. We find the phrase *fear of God* regularly in Scripture, particularly throughout the Old Testament. Exodus 20:20 provides an interesting instance. Moses said to the people, *"Do not be afraid. God has come to test you, so that the fear of God will be with you to keep you from sinning."* The people feared judgment but their reverence and respect for God, based on His own holy character and otherness, would guide them to righteous living.

12. A. W. Tozer, *The Pursuit of God* (Camp Hill, PA: Christian, 1982), 35.

13. Frank Laubach, *Letters by a Modern Mystic* (New York: New Readers Press, 1955), quoted in Richard Foster and James Bryan Smith, *Devotional Classics* (New York: HarperCollins, 1993), 119.

14. Taylor, *When God Is Silent,* 51.

15. C. S. Lewis, Brainy Quote, *www.brainyquote.com/quotes/authors/ c/c_s_lewis.html.*

16. Ibid.

17. Quoted by Richard Innes, "On Being Heavenly Minded," Acts International, *www.actsweb.org/articles/article.php?i=1553&d=2&c=2.*

Chapter 4

1. C. Colpe, "The Sacred and the Profane," *The Encyclopedia of Religion* (New York: MacMillan, 1987), Vol. 12, 513–14.

2. J. R. Schroeder and J. Aust, "Cursing More Prevalent on American TV," *World News and Trends,* (Nov/Dec 2003), *www.ucgstp.org/ lit/gn/gn049/worldnews.htm.*

3. See Exodus 19:5–6: " 'Although the whole earth is mine, you will be for me *a kingdom of priests and a holy nation.*' These are the words you are to speak to the Israelites."

4. W. E. Vine, *Vine's Expository Dictionary of Old and New Testament Words* (Grand Rapids, MI: Revell, 1981), 190.

5. The precise origin of the Pharisaic movement in Jesus' day remains a little clouded, but many scholars believe that the movement arose in the third century BC as a holiness movement devoted to maintaining Jewish purity and observing the Jewish Law as a means to restore God's favor and the land to Israel.

6. See, too, Revelation 1:5–6: "To him who loves us and has freed us from our sins by his blood, and has made us to be *a kingdom and priests* to serve his God and Father—to him be glory and power for ever and ever! Amen." Also, Revelation 5:10: "You have made them to be a *kingdom and priests* to serve our God, and they will reign on the earth."

7. *Jesus* is the Greek form of the Hebrew name *Joshua,* which means "The LORD saves."

8. Those issues include the challenges of genetic research, stem-cell research, military engagement in a world where weaponry has unparalleled sophistication, global warming, global poverty, HIV/AIDS, and Web pornography.

9. See "Women in Greek and Roman Egypt," Women in the Ancient World, *www.womenintheancientworld.com/greek%20and%20 roman%20egypt.htm*. We measure the modern infant mortality rate by the number of deaths of children under one year of age, per one thousand births. In 2001, the world rate dropped to its best level on record, fifty-seven (or 5.7 percent)—though Sierra Leone in Africa had a rate of 157 (or 15.7 percent). For a more comprehensive table, see "Mortality, Infant," *Encyclopedia of Death and Dying* (July 31, 2007): *www.deathreference.com/Me-Nu/ Mortality-Infant.html*. See too, Valerie French, "Midwives and Maternity Care in the Roman World," Indiana University, *www. indiana.edu/~ancmed/midwife.HTM,* in which she notes: "The death of a woman or her baby was an all-too-common occur-rence. Caesar's daughter Julia died in childbirth. The younger Pliny reports that both daughters of one of his friends, Helvidius, died during labor. And the Athenian philanthropist, Herodes Atticus, was grief-stricken when his first child, a son, died on the day of his birth. The anxiety and grief of the elite was surely paralleled among the lower classes."

10. Eric Scheske, "St. Gregory of Nyssa," Catholic.Net, *www.catholic. net/RCC/Periodicals/Faith/2000–910/scheske.html*.

11. Gregory of Nyssa, *The Life of Moses* (San Francisco: Harper-SanFrancisco, 2006), 5.

12. Thomas à Kempis, *The Imitation of Christ,* trans., William C. Creasy (Notre Dame, IN: Ave Maria, 2001), 134.

13. William Law, *A Serious Call to a Devout and Holy Life* (New York: Random House, 2002), 6.

Chapter 5

1. "Alexander the Great Quotes," ThinkExist.com, *http://thinkexist. com/quotation/do-you-not-think-it-a-matter-worthy-of/360868.html.*

2. Morris Stuart, *So Long, Farewell, and Thanks for the Church* (Sydney, Australia: Hodder & Stoughton, 1992), 44, notes that in Genesis 1:27, we see an equality between man and woman that disappears after the fall so that men and women constantly seek to exercise dominion over one another. "To the image are now added the dimensions of counterfeit and contradiction. Counterfeit, because the human creature after the fall no longer appears simply 'after the image and likeness of God.' Now with the advent of sin, the human creature strives to be as a god. Contradiction, because that which originally appeared as an image, a reflection of the Godhead in whom there is equality, diversity, and unity, now appears as a hierarchy. This is indeed the marring of the image. The human creature now contradicts the nature of its creator, and distorts the image."

3. John Calvin, *Golden Booklet of the True Christian Life,* trans., Henry J. Van Andel (Grand Rapids, MI: Baker Books, 2005), 32.

4. D. A. Carson in *The Sermon on the Mount* (Carlisle, UK: Paternoster, 1994), 63, writes: "It ensures that our giving is not prompted, even in part, by a love for the praise of peers. No one will know what we have given; and, if there is a danger that secret pride will be nurtured, we ourselves are scarcely to know what we've given. . . ." Walter Luthi and Robert Brunner cleverly write in *The Sermon on the Mount* (Edinburgh, UK: Oliver & Boyd, 1963), 89: "What you give must remain in one hand: it must not even be passed from the right hand to the left. Above all it must not go to your head!"

5. "The Oprah Winfrey Show," Wikipedia, *http://en.wikipedia.org/ wiki/Oprah_Winfrey_Show*. Jon Bon Jovi had at that time sold 100 million albums over the span of his career.

6. Business Process Trends, *www.bptrends.com/resources_glossary. cfm?wordid=1585D3FD-1031-D522–3C41C050AD12C6DA*. Patrick Lencioni develops the metaphor very nicely in his book *Silos, Politics, and Turf Wars* (San Francisco: Jossey-Bass, 2006), where he applies the phrase to his analysis of organizational life.

Chapter 6

1. Interestingly, Jesus uses the singular form of *heaven* in this instance rather than the plural form *heavens* (v. 9) that we examined in chapter 3. He obviously intends to set up a contrast between "heaven and earth," and His hearers would likely have understood "the third heaven" (or the spiritual heaven) from the context. The use of the singular in this verse reinforces the significance of the plural form used earlier.

2. Calvin, *Golden Booklet of the True Christian Life*, 55.

3. Brennan Manning, *Ruthless Trust: The Ragamuffin's Path to God* (New York: HarperCollins, 2000), 5.

4. Bonhoeffer, *Life Together*, 27.

5. James Collins and Jerry Porras first proposed the phrase BHAG— Big Hairy Audacious Goal—in their article "Building Your Company's Vision," *Harvard Business Review* (Sept. 1, 1996). A BHAG (BEE-hag) is "an audacious 10-to-30-year goal to progress toward an envisioned future. . . . A true BHAG is clear and compelling, serves as a unifying focal point of effort, and acts as a clear catalyst for team spirit." Collins and Porras later used this concept in their book *Built to Last: Successful Habits of Visionary Companies* (New York: HarperCollins, 2004).

6. *Peaceful Warrior* is an American film starring Scott Mechlowicz, Nick Nolte, and Amy Smart. Released on June 2, 2006, it is based on the novel *Way of the Peaceful Warrior* by Dan Millman.

7. "Thomas Merton Quotes," Brainy Quote, *www.brainyquote.com/quotes/authors/t/thomas_merton.html*.

8. Henri Nouwen, *Adam: God's Beloved* (Maryknoll, NY: Orbis, 1997), 84.

9. Consider also Philippians 2:12–13: "Therefore, my dear friends, as you have always obeyed—not only in my presence, but now much more in my absence—continue to work out your salvation with fear and trembling, for it is God who works in you to will and to act according to his good purpose." Paul does not dismiss the need for believers to work, but that work must conform to God's will and purpose and no longer our own.

10. "To keep me from becoming conceited because of these surpassingly great revelations, there was given me a thorn in my flesh, a messenger of Satan, to torment me. Three times I pleaded with the Lord to take it away from me. But he said to me, 'My grace is sufficient for you, for my power is made perfect in weakness.' Therefore I will boast all the more gladly about my weaknesses, so that Christ's power may rest on me" (2 Corinthians 12:7–9).

11. Nouwen, *Adam,* 83.

Chapter 7

1. Reuters Report, "New Inflation Warning for Zimbabwe," 7/31/2007, *www.cnn.com/2007/BUSINESS/07/31/imf.zimbabwe.reut/index.html*. Compare the 4.1 percent inflation rate for the U.S. in 2007.

2. Wright, *The Lord and His Prayer,* 36.

3. Dale C. Allison, *The Sermon on the Mount: Inspiring the Moral Imagination* (New York: Crossroad, 1999), 125.

4. Eugene Peterson covers this well. *Eat This Book: A Conversation in the Art of Spiritual Reading* (Grand Rapids, MI: Eerdmans, 2006), 147–50. See also, William J. Carl, *The Lord's Prayer for Today* (Louisville, KY: Westminster, 2006), 49–55.

5. George Morrison, *Classic Sermons on the Lord's Prayer,* ed., Warren Wiersbe (Grand Rapids, MI: Kregel, 2000), 104.

6. Paul Hiebert, "The Flaw of the Excluded Middle," *Missiology,* Vol. 10, Issue 1 (January 1982): 35–47. In more recent times, John Mark Ministries has suggested that the pendulum has swung so far that the danger is a flaw of an *expanded* middle in which every strange event is thought to have a middle domain explanation. *http://jmm.aaa.net.au/articles/14692.htm.*

7. Docetism (from the Greek *dokeo,* "to seem, or have the appearance of") argued that "if Christ suffered he was not divine, and if he was God he could not suffer." See G. L. Borchert, "Docetism" in *Evangelical Dictionary of Theology* (Grand Rapids, MI: Baker, 1992), 326.

8. Gnosticism (from the Greek *ginosko,* "to know") emphasized secret spiritual knowledge as the pathway to enlightenment. It likely sprung from a philosophical combination of Platonism and Christianity. Plato taught in the fourth century BC that everything we see is an inferior reproduction of the true Ideal that exists in the spiritual realm. It doesn't take much for those who hold such a philosophical worldview to begin to believe that this world, which the Lord will one day destroy with fire, is inherently corrupt and therefore *un*spiritual. This sequence of thinking is deeply damaging to our Christian worldview.

9. See, for example, the heavy emphasis at the beginning of 1 John on John's experience of Christ, the One whom we have "heard . . . seen . . . looked upon . . . handled . . . seen . . . seen and heard. . ." (1 John 1:1–3 KJV). Later John urges his readers to "test the spirits

to see whether they are from God. . . . Every spirit that confesses that Jesus Christ *has come in the flesh* is from God" (1 John 4:1–2 NASB).

10. Willimon and Hauerwas, *Lord, Teach Us*, 75.

11. In the original Greek, the term translated "daily" (*epiousion*) occurs only in this one place in the whole New Testament. For centuries scholars scratched their heads as to its meaning. Did it perhaps allude to a very special kind of bread? In the late nineteenth century, archeological digs in Egypt unearthed some ancient shopping lists that used the same word. The mystery was finally solved and the term lost its mystical aura.

12. "Greed Quotes," ThinkExist.com, *http://thinkexist.com/quotations/greed*.

13. "How We Can Live Simply in the Twenty-First Century," Christian Simple Living, *www.christiansimpleliving.org/BraveDareNot.htm*.

14. Cited in Willimon and Hauerwas, *Lord, Teach Us*, 76.

Chapter 8

1. Simon Wiesenthal, *The Sunflower: On the Possibilities and Limits of Forgiveness* (New York: Schocken Books, 1998).

2. Paul Tournier, *Guilt and Grace* (New York: Hodder & Stoughton, 1962), 192.

3. "Emo Philips Quotes," ThinkExist.com, *http://thinkexist.com/quotation/when_i_was_a_kid_i_used_to_pray_every_night_for_a/155486.html*.

4. Willard, *The Divine Conspiracy*, 57.

5. Tozer, *The Pursuit of God*, 42.

6. Ibid., 44–45.

Chapter 9

1. Many translations—NIV, NASB, KJV, ESV, and others—choose to translate this passage with the word *tempted*. This word choice creates confusion for us later. I'd prefer to see the word *tested*.

2. *Peirasmos* is the noun; *peiradzo* is the verb. The root is the same for both.

3. Carson, *The Sermon on the Mount*, 78, writes: "Lead us, not into temptation, but away from it, into righteousness, into situations where, far from being tempted, we will be protected and therefore kept righteous." Wright, *The Lord and His Prayer*, 73, also suggests that this phrase might have meant: "Let us escape the great tribulation, the great testing, that is coming on all the world."

4. Gordon MacDonald, "Leader's Insight: When Leaders Implode," *Christianity Today*, www.christianitytoday.com/leaders/newsletter/2006/cln61106.html.

5. William Shakespeare, *Hamlet* (New York: Penguin Classics, 2001), III, ii, 239.

6. "AA Fact File," Alcoholics Anonymous, www.alcoholics-anonymous.org/en_information_aa.cfm?PageID=2.

7. A drachma was approximately a day's wage, so 50,000 days' wages was the income for about 137 years. The equivalent today would be quite staggering.

8. Jerry Bridges, *The Pursuit of Holiness* (Colorado Springs: NavPress, 1982), 84.

9. Ibid., 20.

10. David Timms, "Presidents . . . About Life," *The LOOKOUT* (January 6, 2008).

Chapter 10

1. The final words of the Lord's Prayer—"for yours is the kingdom, the power, and the glory unto the ages. Amen."—first appear in a manuscript from the fifth century, then regularly in manuscripts from the ninth to the eleventh centuries. While many translations footnote the words, they represent a long tradition within the church.

2. Caleb Kaltenbach, one of my graduate students, shared these warming reflections in an online course (*Dynamics of Servant Leadership*) that I taught in fall 2007.

3. Jean-Pierre de Caussade in Foster and Smith, *Devotional Classics*, 232.

Chapter 11

1. Eugene Peterson, *The Jesus Way* (Grand Rapids, MI: Eerdmans, 2007), 261.

2. Eugene Peterson, *Reversed Thunder* (San Francisco: Harper & Row, 1988), 69.

3. Ibid., 68–69.

4. Not all of the ancient manuscripts of Matthew's gospel conclude with the word *Amen*, though many do.

5. Helen Roseveare, *Living Sacrifice* (London, UK: Hodder & Stoughton, 1979), 96–97.

6. Associated Press, "Report: Lockheed Martin Failed to Test Doomed Genesis Space Probe," Fox News, 6/15/07, *www.foxnews.com/story/0,2933,199486,00.html*.

7. Hannah More in Richard Foster and Emilie Griffin, *Spiritual Classics* (New York: HarperCollins, 2000), 348.

8. Ibid.

9. Calvin, *Golden Booklet of the True Christian Life*, 32.

Postscript

1. Frank Laubach, "Meditation on the Lord's Prayer," in *Man of Prayer,* ed., Karen R. Norton (Syracuse, NY: Laubach Literacy Foundation, 1990), 325–26.
2. Henri Nouwen, *The Selfless Way of Christ* (Maryknoll, NY: Orbis, 2007), 35.

David Timms teaches New Testament and Theology and serves as chair of the Graduate Ministry Department at Hope International University in Fullerton, California. Australian by birth, David has been a church planter, pastor, and trainer of pastors for twenty-five years. He publishes an e-zine, *In Hope,* that shares his reflections on Christian leadership and spiritual formation. He and his wife, Kim, have three sons and live in Fullerton, California.

.